The Road to Peace Runs through the Valley of Death

How to Be Your Own Shaman

PAUL GREENBAUM

Healing from the Heart Publishing

The Road to Peace Runs through the Valley of Death

© 2016 Paul Greenbaum

All rights reserved. No part of this book may be used or reproduced in any manner whatsoever without written permission except in the case of brief quotations embodied in critical articles and reviews.

HEALING FROM THE HEART PUBLISHING
916 SE 70th Ave
Portland, Oregon 97215
503-319-3573
paulgreenbaum@comcast.net

Edition ISBNs
Trade Paperback: 978-0-9796483-2-8
E-book: 978-0-9796483-6-6

First Edition 2016

This edition was prepared for printing by
The Editorial Department
7650 E. Broadway, #308
Tucson, Arizona 85710
www.editorialdepartment.com

Book interior design by Morgana Gallaway

To my lovely wife Jeeranan

Contents

PART 1: Overview — 1

  Chapter 1: *The Search for Fulfillment* — 3

  Chapter 2: *Paul's Story* — 13

  Chapter 3: *Not Unique* — 23

PART 2: Open Your Inner Eyes — 33

  Chapter 4: *Light the Flame of the Inner Heart* — 35

  Chapter 5: *Finding the Inner Self* — 41

PART 3: The Fall from Grace (How the Mind Became Master) — 59

  Chapter 6: *Banished from the Garden of Eden* — 61

  Chapter 7: *Splitting the Mind with Fear, Greed, and Guilt* — 71

PART 4: Unlearning — 93

  Chapter 8: *Not Therapy* — 95

  Chapter 9: *Know Thyself: . . . That Is, Know the Small Self* — 111

  Chapter 10: *Going Deeper with the Fast Path* — 127

PART 5: Unraveling the Glue of the Ego — 135

  Chapter 11: *Unconscious Shock* — 137

  Chapter 12: *Subtle Levels of Shock* — 153

PART 6: Understanding Our Coping Mechanisms	169
Chapter 13: *Shunting (Getting Away from the Mind)*	171
Chapter 14: *Dark Meditation*	177
PART 7: Piercing Shock	199
Chapter 15: *The Secret Place of the Most High*	201
Chapter 16: *Rites of Passage (The External Approach)*	209
PART 8: Surrender and Awakening	223
Chapter 17: *Surrender*	225
Chapter 18: *Seeing With Different Eyes*	241
POSTSCRIPT	257

*Before we can understand our own soul,
we must explore all that eclipses our true selves.*

—B.K.S. Iyengar

PART 1

Overview

Chapter 1

The Search for Fulfillment

WHAT DO YOU WANT?

Go to the best life coaches in the world and that's probably the first question they'll ask. The answer most people give is some version of being happy, thin, adored, healthy, or wealthy. But if you could fast-forward to your deathbed, would you have the same desires—and even if you attained them, would you be satisfied?

When you're at death's door, having the perfect figure or the perfect bank account amounts to zero. And if the entire world adored you, would you even believe it? Might there be anything else you would've liked to do with your life?

As a teenager, I almost died from a drug overdose. As the cocaine traveled through my arteries, my heart pounded wildly. I collapsed to the ground with a crushing pain in my chest and intense panic, which was soon replaced by absolute calm. It was indescribably weird, but at the same time as natural as the rising of the sun. My drug-filled body felt violated and my mind was in turmoil, but some inner part of me calmly watched—awake, alive, and crystal clear. This part knew everything about my life; it was the faculty that allowed my life to "pass" before my eyes—and clearly, I'd missed the boat. I'd done nothing meaningful, was more of a leech, taking from the host of life but giving back very little. I'd been alive but hadn't lived. Somehow I'd built a cage around me to insulate and protect my heart. I was too afraid to allow myself to receive much love. Inside I was starving. As I faced that it might be my time to leave, I felt acute remorse. More than anything, I wished I could have another chance.

One thing can be said with absolute certainty: when it comes time to die, you're going to want to have lived. You will want to have reached your full potential and lived the fullest life possible. Sadly, most never do. When the scant few years of a lifetime have slipped away, one is often left with regrets, wrong choices, and unattained desires. And though unfulfilled, one is often still afraid to leave this life.

Why are we afraid of death?

From a very young age we're taught to seek fulfillment outside ourselves. Many years are spent building our separate lives: educating ourselves, developing our personalities, working, seeking love and recognition, and attempting to amass our big bank balances. Of course, building our outer lives is necessary, but it may not be enough to bring real peace and fulfillment.

For example, take a couple who actually achieved the so-called "American dream." As a teenager, the man couldn't help but notice that the lovely women in television and magazine commercials always wore beautiful clothes and surrounded themselves with expensive possessions. He figured the best way to get good-looking women was to become rich and powerful, and so he put forth the strength of his heart and soul and created a fortune.

The woman had been a gorgeous model with many suitors, and her mother always said it's just as easy to marry a rich man as a poor one, and infinitely better in the long run. She knew that her beauty gave her an advantage in marrying at the top of the food chain.

And so it was love at first sight, or it seemed like love. They fulfilled each other's desires. They traveled the world, had plenty of sex, and settled into a beautiful home with a couple of kids. On the outside they had realized their dreams, yet each of them still had a nagging feeling that there should be more to life. However, neither had any idea what that "more" was or how to find it.

As the years passed, the woman's beauty began to fade. Men stopped looking at her, including her husband. He started having affairs with younger, now more beautiful women.

After the divorce, both people tried to continue with the

only ways they knew. The man, though he'd become fat and needed sex-enhancing drugs to perform, was still able to attract beautiful women who exchanged sex for material support. But then one day, he had a massive heart attack. On his deathbed, he realized that all he'd done with his life was make money. None of the many women he'd slept with, including his wife, had ever loved him, probably because he never let himself love anyone. He died with a full bank account, but inside he was a beggar.

The woman tried to regain her beauty with liposuction and plastic surgery. The facelift smoothed out her wrinkles, but everyone could see she was just trying to shore up a sinking ship. All she'd ever had was outer beauty; when it faded, she seemed to be left with nothing. She became depressed and started taking medication. She developed health problems and died a bitter, fearful person.

If fulfillment comes from riches, what happens if they're taken away? If happiness is dependent on someone's loving us, what happens when it changes? If we are pleased because we are young, beautiful, and healthy, what happens when those conditions pass? If happiness comes from being held up as special, what will happen when we lose favor? Enjoy every gift that life has to offer, sure. But focusing only on the impermanent—what must change—is like building castles in the sand.

The funny thing is, as the years pass, we start believing that the sand castles are solid and real. We try to protect them, but no matter how well we insulate ourselves from change, no safe place exists in the outer world. When a big wave hits, sand castles return to the sea. Everything is passing. Fortunes rise and fall, the most powerful man gets weak, the greatest beauty fades, and the most passionate love cools. There is no talisman, prayer, or antidote against change, and death is always waiting. When death knocks, we must leave all that we've spent a lifetime building. That's why there's fear. We latch on to what can't be held; we try to protect and control that which can't be controlled or protected. If our outer identities—body, mind, and emotion—are all there is, there has to be fear, especially as we age and lose power. If we think we are only the mind and body, then death is the end of everything.

Yogis, sages, and meditation masters say that before one dies, one must taste death—become familiar with the part of oneself that doesn't die, the part we take with us. Only if we have tasted death, they say, can we truly live. But we're not trained to embrace and explore death, or to understand what that even means.

Death is the inevitable end—but of what? Imagine the death experience as being much like sitting on your favorite chair, looking around the house before leaving on a long, far-away trip. It's time to say good-bye to everything and everyone, but this time there are no bags to pack, and you're not coming back to sit in your favorite chair ever again. Whatever you've done here is finished. As the dying process ensues, there is the inevitable letting go of the physical body and mind, and a complete surrender into an unknown.

To taste death before you die, you surrender the ego, your separate self. It requires the same letting go into an unknown as does real death and leads to the experience of oneness with life while still alive—an awakening into reality. Unlike therapies, self-help, spiritual belief systems, and trying to love oneself, this awakening is a true game-changer. When you see that you are deathless, an immortal drop of pure love, fear evaporates. Being one with life brings freedom and contentment that can't be found in the outer world. You, your nervous system, and the way you approach life will never be the same.

The Non-dual State

Some awakened masters tell us that anything that changes is not real: we're not born, nor do we die, and the body and mind are illusions. On the deepest level this is true, but frequently, even these masters' own disciples don't understand what they're talking about. Perhaps that's because the masters speak from a place of non-duality: the undifferentiated source, the place where life is eternal and unchanging. To dwell there is to live in bliss. Ramakrishna, a sage who lived in the 1900s, entered so deeply into states of ecstasy that he could barely function. His disciples had to tend to his bodily needs. When one attains a non-dualistic state, one can stay in bliss for long periods of time. It may even be possible to hide out there.

Not One or the Other

It's not the outer world *or* the inner world that brings fulfillment, but bringing both together in the ever-present now. Awakening isn't a one-sided denial of human life. It's not the lukewarm reality of waiting until you die so you never have to be born again. To awaken is to live absolutely fully.

I think of a story from the Tao about Lao Tzu, Taoism's founder. The king had heard that Lao Tzu was a great sage who understood the workings of the universe. The king sent a retinue of men to comb the countryside and bring Lao Tzu back to serve in his cabinet. But where to find him? Lao Tzu had no home; he lived naked in the wilderness. Supposedly, the animals brought him food and lay against him at night to keep him warm. (All of life will serve one who has fully surrendered to life. That person's needs will be taken care of, without his having to toil for sustenance.)

After much searching, they found Lao Tzu naked, sunning himself on the banks of a river. The men told Lao Tzu of his good fortune: the king wanted him to serve in the government. But Lao Tzu pointed to a huge turtle sitting in the mud and said, "Do you think that turtle would rather be stuffed and preserved, brought back to your court and placed in a fine cabinet . . . or would he rather stay here wagging his tail in the mud?"

"I would think this turtle would much rather stay here by the river," a servant replied.

Lao Tzu laughed. "Then you be gone and leave this old turtle."

Like Lao Tzu, I'm all about wagging my tail in the mud.

After awakening, you can understand that you and life (what most people call God) are not separate but one. You will know that the real self is pure love, the substance behind all life. Freedom exists because you have your roots in the unchanging soul of the universe, but that only serves to enhance the celebration of life.

A famous Zen koan says: "Before awakening chop wood, carry water. After awakening chop wood, carry water." Before awakening you search and struggle in the outer world, but fulfillment eludes you. After awakening you perform the same tasks and duties, but now all of life—both pain and pleasure—is a profound gift. You may still have struggles in the outer world, but the inner struggle is over, and so is the search. You've found what you were looking for: yourself.

Why wait for death to come knocking? If you can't find peace, gratitude, and bliss within your own skin in the here and now, what guarantee is there that it will be waiting for you at death, in the future, or in another dimension? No one can make such a claim, and so those who have sought truth have looked not only to scriptures, belief systems, or yoga postures but also to discovering how to live in peace, joy, and gratitude—right now.

I'm not a Christian, Muslim, Buddhist, Jew, Hindu, Taoist, or a member of any other religion. I don't follow any particular path, because each path is only one viewpoint, like looking through a hole in a fence. You may see something, but not the whole picture. This book embraces knocking the entire fence down so that nothing blocks the view.

The title—*The Road to Peace Runs through the Valley of Death*—was inspired by my interpretation of Psalm 23:4: "Yea, though I walk through the valley of the shadow of death, I will fear no evil; For You are with me; Your rod and Your staff, they comfort me."

The valley of death is your mind, and heaven and hell are within you. Don't worry about meeting devils with pitchforks, either now or in the afterlife. You will find your demons (obstacles to awakening) lurking within your own mind.

Before you can get to the point of surrender, you must pass through the valley of death to your very core. But have no fear. Your true self, the inner guru, the god within, is always with you.

The first part of this book will give you an overview of the awakening experience. Subsequent sections will take you progressively deeper inside yourself, through the layers of your mind, en route to the core. As you go, you'll find exercises intended to help you develop your ever-increasing awareness, leading ultimately to surrender.

Chapter 2

Paul's Story

Overdosing on cocaine, coming near death that first time, was my first glimpse of reality—or at least the first one I could recall at the time. For a day afterward, I was quietly and humbly astonished. Then I forgot all about the part of me that was crystal clear and alive and tried to return to my old life, but it had gone strangely sour. I couldn't use drugs with the same careless abandon. They fell away naturally, through no effort on my part. Something had indelibly shifted. Though I wasn't consciously aware of it, I became a hound looking for a fresh scent. I wanted to find the part of me that was so blissfully *alive*.

Soon after, I met a man who changed my life. His martial arts class was like sunshine breaking through a socked-in day, his kung fu the most beautiful thing I'd ever seen. I had to learn and soon became completely absorbed in study. The drugs stopped. I moved from New York City to upstate New York to be closer to my teacher. Martial arts, yoga, meditation, and a committed spiritual path became my new drugs, and I devoted all my time to practice.

Many tools in these disciplines were useful and positive. Yoga brought health and flexibility to my body. Through martial arts, I became a capable fighter. With meditation, I could stop my thoughts and reach a state of deep and blissful quiet. Yet I never found the underlying gift these practices promised: awakening. Peace, bliss, joy, and love were what I was really looking for.

By the time I was twenty-one, I'd read hundreds of spiritual books. Intellectually, I knew all about the spiritual path. But it wasn't until many years later, once I had the actual experience of becoming one with life, that I understood the common thread between these books.

First, however, came a long struggle.

In my mid-twenties, death knocked on my door a second time. I woke up one morning with pain in my chest, a spinning head, and such exhaustion I could barely drag myself to my feet. I lay down on the cabin floor and couldn't get up. Again I came into contact with the part of me that was so vibrantly alive, the part that knew every detail of truth about me. As I faced death this time, only three things were important: Had

I given and received enough love? Had I done what I came here to do? Was I leaving the world a better place than I'd found it? For a second time I took stock of my life and for a second time came up short. Inside, however, something had been activated and was moving in the right direction. Then I lost consciousness.

The emergency-room doctors thought I'd had a ministroke. My resting heartbeat had gone from forty beats per minute to over one hundred. It was more than a little strange, but in the medical world I'd peaked just over the high side of normal, which is ninety beats per minute. After visiting my regular doctor and doing a battery of tests, I'd still found nothing tangibly wrong with me.

I was referred from cardiologist to gastroenterologist and through a long line of specialists. After even more extensive tests, the gastroenterologist thought he saw a questionable twist of my intestine that might be cancerous. The cardiologist also thought he saw something suspicious. Still, no one could put a finger on anything, and I had no more money for further testing.

My fatigue was so great that anything—even standing on my feet—sapped my energy. I couldn't count on myself to have the power to do anything. I became hypersensitive. Even common noises like rain or a ticking clock bothered me, and I had trouble sleeping for the first time in my life. Worst were the crippling panic attacks that made even leaving the house difficult. I'd never experienced such fear. Why now? At the time, I didn't understand that there's fear inside us all. It's only when we're ready to face it that it begins to surface. But I wasn't ready, and I continued to try to push it away.

It was such a strange place to be. Life was blooming all around me. My buddies were progressing with their martial arts; others were building their professions or spending time with family or girlfriends. I was forced to take a hiatus. For more than two years, I dropped out of life and let everything pass me by. I was twenty-five and I should've been a superman, but I felt like an old man, and a washed-up one at that. I didn't know I was passing through what some have called a spiritual crisis. Though at an extremely low point, I vowed that someday, somehow, I'd come back. I'd find a way to live fully.

So began an intense quest to get well. I experimented with nutrition, biofeedback, herbs, hydrotherapy, homeopathy, and colonics. I learned how to use tai chi, *qigong*, meditation, and yoga to heal. I completely devoted myself to the practice. Slowly, as the months passed, my energy improved, and I started taking long walks outside.

I still couldn't practice hard martial arts, so to pass the time, I went to the local university to learn anatomy, physiology, and Chinese, which would be useful when I returned to the martial arts. I ended up deciding to be a doctor.

After eleven years of school, I had three licenses: for

chiropractic, acupuncture, and massage therapy. My practice was an immediate success, but then a patient came in who cried every time she got onto my table. I didn't know what to do. One day she came in for her appointment at four o'clock, and when I left work at seven, she was still sitting on the steps, tears rolling down her face. I referred her to a therapist, but I knew that if I was going to become a well-rounded healer, I had to learn more about mind-body medicine.

Life's funny that way: I believed my motivation was to help others, but in truth I was still reaching toward figuring myself out. So began more than a decade of study in the non-physical side of healing. I studied dozens of therapies: esoteric psychology, color and light therapies, Thought Field Therapy, and a long list of others. Among the most notable was Bert Hellinger's Family Constellations work, which shed light on the power of the family soul. In rebirthing and pre- and perinatal psychology, I did hundreds of regressions and remembered my birth and time in the womb. But although these systems are brilliant in explaining the source of our deep psychic wounds, their methods of cure fall short. Knowing the cause of our problems isn't the answer. It simply makes the disease more ingrained. It's only when the inner self sees the truth that change happens effortlessly.

Burned out with the mental-ness of psychology, I started spending long periods meditating in solitude. I ate very little and sat by the river. In the silence of nature, I saw just how disturbed and disturbing my mind was. No wonder I had no idea who Paul Greenbaum was. In fact, there was no real Paul Greenbaum—only an ego conditioned by parents, society, religion, and even advertising. I saw clearly that nothing in the mind is new or original. It's more like a backed-up toilet. The same old crap floats around time and time again, endlessly, never getting flushed, and it stinks every time. Hearing the same fears, insecurities, aspirations, and visions of glory day after day made me sick and afraid. It was like a crowd of conflicted people arguing inside me. But the more I observed it, the less real it seemed and the less I identified with it.

In my forties, I met an energy healer who taught me the practical side of going inside. She implored me to stay energetically grounded in my body, and if I slipped out, she constantly reminded me to get back in. Though she didn't give much instruction as to what staying inside the body meant or what leaves when you're not in your body, I eventually learned she was referring to clear consciousness: the alive part I'd discovered when coming near death. Finding this part is the first real step on the path.

The practice of staying in the body required developing an entire new set of energetic "muscles." I found that like most people, I was out of the body as much or more than I was in. Being outside the body makes for a fragmented and stressful existence. When I forced myself to stay inside, I felt the gritty edges of my wounds, an inner chaos, which was, of course, the trigger to leave in the first place. I practiced holding myself in my body as much as possible.

Going through a divorce amped up the process. During emotional turmoil, it was much more challenging to keep myself in the body, but I put tremendous effort into it. When I woke up in the middle of the night deep in anger, sadness, or worry, I didn't distract myself or shunt the intensely uncomfortable emotions. *Shunt* means to move aside or get out of the way. Blood can be diverted and electricity bypassed through a shunt. In his book *The Karate Sensei*, American karate master Peter Urban uses *shunt* to describe avoiding or diverting thoughts and feelings that would be better faced. I use Urban's definition in this book.

Instead of getting away from my pain, I brought myself back to my body and deeper and deeper into the emotion. Eventually, I learned to bring my inner self into the very epicenter of the feeling. It was like finding the eye of a hurricane, a calm oasis in the middle of a raging storm. All around me was turbulent emotional energy that had the potential to activate me and pull me out of the body, but at its core was freedom. I saw that whatever was going on in my mind—even fear—had no power to touch me.

Yet as I became energetically stronger and able to handle seeing more of the chaos inside me, deep elemental fear began to rise from my unconscious mind. I had nothing to be afraid of, and yet I was afraid of the fear itself—or my mind's reaction to it. I spent even more time in solitude outside. With nothing to distract myself, I saw just how crazy my mind could become. If the voice in my head didn't shut up, I was sure I would soon lose my mind; this in turn filled me with more fear. Then there was the other side of the coin: times my mind shut off and left a great silence that first felt peaceful but then felt as if I were dissolving. If I let myself go, I would cease to exist, and this evoked fear. This time, however, I was ready to face whatever came up.

One particular time in the forest, my mind seemed especially harsh. Every thought sent spasms of tension throughout my nervous system. If my mind didn't stop, I thought, I would surely go insane. I tried my usual method of bringing myself inside my body, but this time it didn't work. The very act of bringing myself inside took a terribly jarring effort. I could find no escape from my mind, and I felt backed against a wall. In meditation, this is sometimes called standing at the edge of the cliff. And it's just like being at the end of a gangplank, swords at your back. It's either jump or die. I had to either surrender and let go completely or shunt and forever be tortured by my mind. When I let go, the sensation felt like jumping into a river with the most powerful current; I simply gave up all inner struggle and let the current take me. Instantly, I experienced total bliss and peace. I was one with life: a pure awareness. Only the slightest trace of Paul Greenbaum, my ego-self, remained.

After the surrender it all clicked: it wasn't necessary to toil. Toiling is struggling, allowing the mind to be in charge, to actually listen to the absurd nonsense floating around and allow it to have authority over me. It was my choice. I didn't have to keep re-creating chaos unless I wanted to. I could live in peace.

Some meditation masters describe awakening as permanent, irreversible bliss, free from duality, desire, and fear. It's even common to grade awakening in terms of greater, lesser, and ultimate degrees of attainment. Perhaps my experience was a lesser one. The ego still follows me around, but it's a mere shadow of what it was. I don't claim to be a master of anything or to have achieved an exalted state of consciousness. I'm certainly far from perfect. There's a great deal more I don't know than I do. Even if my experience gave me only the merest glimpse of reality, it has left me centered in my body in peace—and indescribably grateful. Life is a gift that provides everything I need.

If I were called to die now, I could go with the satisfaction of having been so filled with love I'm bursting at the seams. I've done at least a small part of what I came here to do and will leave the world a better place. And when it is time to die, I'll already know how to surrender into the great stream of life.

Chapter 3

Not Unique

Okay, sure, you might be saying. Maybe this guy had an awakening experience, but what does it have to do with me? Despite some personal variations, what happened to me is the same phenomenon described by many paths; no matter what the name or how apparently different the method, the inner stages and energetic results are remarkably similar. There is no way to avoid going inside, through the demons of the mind, to the very core of you.

In kundalini tantra, the goal is to activate and raise the kundalini energy that lies in the base of the spine. To accomplish this, one purifies the subtle energy body through yoga postures, powerful breathing techniques, and methods of detoxification. When the chakras and energy vessels have opened and the flow of breath and energy are perfectly balanced in the *ida* and *pingala* (major energy channels on the right and left sides of the body), an internal signal is given. Kundalini rises from the base of the spine, up the center channel. When the kundalini ascends to the crown chakra, one's intelligence is said to increase many times. Unlike most who use only a tiny portion of their latent power, one taps into the full potential of one's brain and life force.

The ultimate ascent of energy to the crown chakra is called "Shakti meeting Siva." Shakti is one's personal energy. Siva is the universal power. When the individual river empties into the sea, one is forever changed. But to purify the chakras and energy vessels is an inward journey. One never knows what's going to happen when the kundalini energy starts to move. One might have boundless excitement and be filled with energy one day, and the next become so depressed and lethargic that he wants to sleep till noon. Countless stories have been recorded of yogis passing through tremendous mental and emotional turmoil, having to face every nuance of themselves in order for the chakras to be purified, the inner knots untangled, and for the energy to rise to the next level en route to the crown.

With Christian saints, the energetic purification process is called the "dark night of the soul," surrender of the self is known as "may God's will be done," and losing the ego into the stream of life is called "becoming one with God." Just read about the lives of the saints to see the conflict, crisis, and soul-searching one goes through before reaching the other side. Christian saints are depicted with an energetic halo around them, signifying that their *qi* has risen to the crown and that they possess the same open energy field as the yogis, Buddhas, and awakened beings of the East.

Buddha's concept of enlightenment employs techniques of inner exploration through meditation. Buddhists find the inner self and then let it go into the void. After the experience of oneness with life, they insist everything is god.

The samurai wore swords on their belts and protected their lords with their lives. A man might be in the pink of health at sunrise and by sunset be sliced down in a puddle of blood. Because of the ever-present possibility of actual death, a warrior became totally aware of the ultimate reality that so many of us forget: every instant may truly be your last, so you'd better appreciate life right now. Bushido, the way of the warrior, ultimately reveals how to be receptive to life.

Native Americans speak of the path of the true human being. To walk this path, they went inside and faced themselves at every turn through sweat lodges, vision quests, and mortal combat.

From saint to murderer, every individual's feet are set on the path of life. Though all of us may be at different places, it's the same road. No matter how different it may look or what circumstance one finds himself in, everyone eventually turns inward, sifts through the chaos of his mind, and separates the real from the false self. With surrender of the false, the barrier that's keeping you from peace, bliss, and stillness falls away. You awaken to the oneness of life. Buddha, Mahavir, Mohammad, Lao Tzu, Krishna, Christ, and countless others walked this road, and sooner or later, so will you.

The Internal Switch

Awakened people can be described as being clear, and people feel good just sitting in their presence. Being clear, however, is not an outer phenomenon but an inner one. Inner knots are untied and the energy field becomes unobstructed. This process happens not only to spiritual masters but also to warriors and people from all walks of life. The same phenomenon occurs regardless of what prayer or meditation is used, whether one is a vegetarian or a meat-eater, and whether one believes in many gods or none at all. Obviously, it's not so much what one does on the outside. Rather an internal flame is lighted, consciousness wakes up on the inside, and the increased energetic activity stirs repressed emotions—obstructions—that are stuck. The process of untangling is rarely smooth and has the potential to severely unbalance one undergoing the transformation. It's the basis of the spiritual struggle.

However, it must be understood that awakening is not a process or a struggle. Awakening happens when the ego gives up all control and manipulation, completely letting go. Surrender, itself, is the spiritual goal. It leads one to effortlessly merge into the soul of the universe and become one with life. Surrender doesn't happen halfway or in degrees. It is all or nothing, which is why we sometimes call surrender "jumping off the cliff" or "crossing the great abyss." The process of untangling, or the spiritual struggle, refers to the path leading up to surrender. The entire purpose of spiritual practice is to get closer to the point where you are capable of taking the jump. There are eight progressions you may pass through on the path leading to surrender:

LIGHT THE FLAME OF SINCERITY: Make an inner, non-intellectual decision that you want truth and freedom more than you want to protect yourself.

ACCEPT: Accept where you are now and be yourself.

DEEPEN AWARENESS: Activate the witness. Discover your inner self and learn to stay in the body. (Keep the awareness of the real self present in the body.)

UNLEARN: Observe the mind until you see the non-reality of it and stop following it like the Pied Piper.

WATCH: Watch the methods you use to distract yourself from your mind.

PENETRATE: Penetrate fear and shock. Shock is the deepest

elemental fear. You learn to enter it and see that your deepest fears are not real.

THE MOMENT OF TRUTH: Either let go to bliss or continue to be tortured by the mind.

SURRENDER: Let go of the self. Like a river emptying into the sea, you become one with life.

Five Transformations

Letting go of the false self and becoming one with life doesn't require knowledge, faith, belief systems, ethics, morals, a high IQ, or a set of ideals. In fact, simpler minds encounter fewer impediments to surrender. But once surrender happens, you'll undergo at least five tangible energetic changes.

The Inner Self Takes Root in the Body

This is the incredible feeling that occurs when your heart, intuition, and receptivity align with the physical body. You are finally at home in your own body and feel at peace in your skin.

The Ego Mind Takes a Permanent Backseat

You see the mind for what it is: a hodgepodge of neuroses, a broken record. You've learned the mind's tricks so well that you simply stop following or paying attention to it. If you have an old senile neighbor who corners you when she sees you and tries to tell you her life story for the ten thousandth time, do you listen intently? Hardly. Similarly, the mind is just telling an old story you've heard many, many times. You've learn the absolute futility in taking that tired drivel seriously. You fire the mind as your master and put in its proper place as a servant.

The mind actually bows to the new arrangement: it pipes down and becomes more silent. Even it knows it's not healthy for it to be in charge. For example, consider a family where there's a single mom raising an eleven-year-old boy. Mom confides everything to her boy, asks his opinion on her personal affairs and how the household should be run. It's not a healthy relationship. No child should have such responsibility. Nor should the mind be given too much authority. If the mother took care of her personal affairs and let the kid be a kid again, the child would breathe a deep sigh of relief and the entire family unit would be healthier. The same is true when the mind relinquishes control and consciousness takes its rightful place as captain of the ship.

With this change of guard, the entire nervous system cools down. Bioelectrically it's less active. One shifts from sympathetic dominance to living more in the parasympathetic state. The sympathetic branch is the get-up-and-go, action-oriented part of the autonomic nervous system. The parasympathetic branch regulates relaxation. The Chinese would call it yin and yang. During yang states, the nerves fire and hormones are secreted so we can take action. Sympathetic or yang dominance, however, has become the modern disease, which is why it's so common to be habitually tense and anxious. In the yin state, the nerves relax and the body regenerates. The yin state is where one heals. Life lived in balance becomes the joy it's meant to be. You rest deeply to repair and rejuvenate your body, and you have plenty of energy.

This concept corresponds perfectly with the findings of Patanjali, the founder of yoga, who spoke of attenuating thought waves. To attenuate thought waves means to diminish their amplitude. Even thousands of years ago, Patanjali realized that thoughts exist in waves. The stronger and more powerful the wave, the more it tightens the nervous system. If the amplitude of the thought wave can be decreased, you move toward relaxation and inner peace. However, the only real way to attenuate your thought waves is to penetrate the inner demons and take the charge off of them, which lessens the reaction of the sympathetic nervous system.

BECOME HEART-CENTERED

You experience peace within yourself—the ability to be a heart-centered, spontaneous person and to know your path in life. With the mind as boss, you're in a perverted relationship with life, as if the court jester ruled the kingdom. The mind analyzes and tries to decide the best course. This is nearly impossible and crazy-making because there are many voices in the head: *yes, no, maybe, what if I do*, and *what if I don't*. The heart, however, possesses only one voice: it simply knows. The natural order of a human being is to spontaneously live through the knowing of the heart. The heart receives visions from life; the mind, as a useful servant, organizes the vision; and the body does the legwork.

Cessation of Toil

You see that your own mind creates your suffering and that you don't need to create conflict unless you choose to do so. You stop fighting with others, yourself, and life itself. You see the futility of the ego's petty little battles, and you don't have to be right anymore. You stop taking yourself so seriously, which probably results in the greatest possible boon to getting along with others and successful intimate relationships. You understand the ridiculousness of trying to control and manipulate life. Surrender allows you to follow the direction in which life is taking you—to let go, relax, and trust again. This has an enormous effect on inner stillness and your subsequent ability to receive from life. When you truly receive, you experience a spontaneous, bubbling gratitude, simply for the privilege of being alive.

Seek a Win-Win in Life Challenges

As a fifth byproduct of experiencing oneness with life, you see that you can't win at the expense of someone else because anything that hurts any aspect of life also hurts you. You don't need a set of moral rules or a code of ethics to do the right thing; spontaneously doing the loving thing becomes natural, simply because you deeply understand and genuinely care.

Such changes are not unique; they'll happen to anyone who has the experience of oneness with life. Thousands of accounts describe the same process. However, many accounts are confusing because they're shrouded with metaphors, symbols, dogma, and religious ideals. They don't explain the energetic reality of the experience.

PART 2

Open Your Inner Eyes

Chapter 4

Light the Flame of the Inner Heart

LIGHTING THE INNER FLAME ISN'T AN INTELLECTUAL decision; the journey starts deep inside you. The flame represents the awakening of your inner awareness as your inner being quickens and stirs as if waking from a long sleep. Even after the flame is lighted, you may not be aware of it. Yet a corner has been turned, your heart is strong enough to withstand the rigors of self-introspection, you're ready to engage on the journey through the valley of death. Once the inner flame is lighted, all of life conspires to give you the conditions you need to transform yourself, both positive and negative. Many patients come to see me in a state of turmoil and they don't know why. Frequently, I find they are entering into the fire of transformation. I tell them they may have earned it. Perhaps on the deepest level, they've even asked for it.

As the seed holds the potential to grow into a mighty tree, we can live a life of celebration, ecstasy, and meaning. However, if living were a mere progression of years, everyone would blossom. When it came time to die, we'd all be full, ready to go. Yet at the end, most people wish for more time. Even after a lifetime, they haven't made a scratch into living. They've postponed or forgotten aliveness, almost as if they've given a drug or caught in a maze.

An eagle is born in an egg; a fetus is encased in a womb. The baby eagle instinctually breaks the shell to eventually glide in the sky. We leave the womb, but soon afterward, another egg forms to protect us—the egg has always been a metaphor for the ego mind. The ego, our identity, insulates and keeps us separate, which is why children are closer to aliveness than most adults. The child ego egg is thin-shelled, barely formed; thus, a child generally feels more wonder and joy than an adult. Time makes the ego stronger. The adult egg gets thicker, more formidable and harder to crack. But all of us must break out of our separate little eggs or we will rot and die in the shell. Inside the shell, one is protected but never quite alive. How can we live life to the fullest when we're trapped, walled off in an isolated little room, never to experience the vastness of the sky?

Possessing life but not being alive has always been the

spiritual conundrum. To soar to our full heights, we must leave the safety of the egg. But breaking from the cage is something you have to earn. Most important, no one can do it for you. A sprout doesn't crack the seed by itself; it must have the right conditions—moisture, heat, and light—to grow.

Human beings break out of their eggs with courage. The most alive times—always—are when you take the risk to crack your boundaries. But to break the protection of the shell, you must embrace fear. The most horrific and frightening things you will ever face are within your own mind. To find peace and inner freedom, you must be willing to go inside and ride out the storm, examine the distortion that's tying you up in knots, and embrace your darkest demons. Most people, however, would rather avoid pain than face it, which makes true awakening the gem it is.

In today's health care, doctors must have patients sign a "Consent to Treat" form. This means the physician must tell patients the risks of treatment and offer alternative therapies that might help. Consent to Treat educates a patient on possible options. Therapists have told me that many patients, when offered the choice of working through their issues or taking medication, opt for the medication. Most prefer to take the easy road out. But on the true spiritual path, that simply doesn't work.

In the book *Magic and Mystery in Tibet*, Alexandra David-Néel witnessed a man performing the ritual of Chöd, which entails sitting in a remote place and offering up one's body and being for hungry ghosts and demons to feast on (a form of surrender). The fellow was in abject terror, as if ghosts and entities were actually consuming him. David-Néel spoke to the lama who was guiding this man and warned him that his student was in significant danger of permanent psychic damage—that he might even die. The lama said the dangers of enlightenment have always been sickness, madness, and even death. Anyone who wishes to walk the road must be ready to face what's inside, including the deepest recesses of fear.

Fear Defines Our Lives

It's absolutely true that fear defines our lives; we build a life around fear and consciously and unconsciously choose activities that don't cast us into waters too deep to swim. But not allowing ourselves to get too far from our comfort zone is living like a mouse in a hole. It's as if we venture out to scout around for a treat, but at the first loud noise we go scampering back to the nest.

Most of us don't live fully. We don't go as far as we might in love, sports, career, spirituality, or any other aspect of life. Fear makes one settle, content to stay on the surface; swimming the depths requires taking a risk. But on your deathbed, you won't regret the mistakes you've made or even the failures. Falling on your face is how you learn. You'll regret only the things you didn't do because you were too afraid to take the chance.

As a young man, I'd enter martial arts tournaments. The host would give the same speech every time in a booming voice while the competitors stood listening. "All you guys are winners," he said. "What happens in your matches doesn't matter. You're winners!"

At the time I didn't understand him. Obviously, some of us would go home without getting our hands raised in triumph. But years later, I finally got it. The losers stayed home because they were too afraid even to show up.

We've lived with ourselves so long we believe our lives are normal, but we don't realize how we've built a life around fear. When activated into pain we find a way to avoid it or distract ourselves from it. Imagine being in your home and you see a burglar climbing through the window and you run away, lock yourself in your bedroom, and turn on the television. Now you don't see the burglar, but a dangerous person is in your house. How will you rest? You know danger exists, and the knowing activates your nervous system. Until you call the police and see the burglar being escorted out of your home, you're going to be anxious no matter what you do to avoid it. That's what we must do with the fear deep inside the mind: look it in the eye until we see it can't hurt us.

Those who are completely satisfied with their lives don't need to do anything. Why should they? No fire has been lighted under them. But if you're anxious, bored, depressed, or otherwise not right inside, it might even be called life's invitation to grow. Pain is the great motivator. Most turn to self-help growth methods or seek the spiritual path through suffering. It's usually when one is beaten down and frustrated by life, when the outer paths are exhausted and one remains unfulfilled, that the inner switch is thrown. A flame is lighted from the inside. A deep unconscious decision is made: you want to live more than you want to protect yourself. Then you are ready to stop looking outside of yourself and go in.

So what will it be for *you*? Are you the sporting type?

Chapter 5

Finding the Inner Self

LIFE BEGINS ANEW WHEN YOU RECOGNIZE THE INNER self—the same clear alive part I found when I came near death. It goes by many names: the witness, child, observer, soul, essence, consciousness, primal intelligence, original face, original innocence, real self, crystal mirror, spirit, atman, non-atman, true being, part that doesn't change, and more. But the name doesn't matter. It's the *real you*—a drop of *pure consciousness*. When you find it, you've found what death can't take. No matter how old you become, this part doesn't age. No matter how sick you may be, this place is not diseased. You may be in great pain and suffering, but this part remains unburdened. No matter how exhausted your body may be, this part never needs rest. Nothing in the outer world can touch it. Nor can the greatest pleasure. The inner self has been compared to the greatest depths of the ocean. On the surface there may be a raging storm—gale-force winds may whip waves a hundred feet high—but when you go to the depths, there is stillness, a place untouched by what's happening on the outside. If you go to the depths of yourself, the place that never changes is always still.

Unlike the mind and body, the inner self always lives in peace and contentment, no matter what the outer circumstances. It is not necessarily happy. Joy and happiness are not permanent. They switch into the opposite polarities of misery and unhappiness. *Bliss* is the word used to describe the inner self. It is neither happy nor unhappy; it is blissfully alive and nothing can change it. It simply is. Life, by its very nature, is always changing. There is no formula, prayer, or talisman to keep you off the roller coaster. The only place of true poise and balance is at rest in the inner self, the place that doesn't change.

An old Tibetan master once said he would be content living anywhere, even in hell. To believe such a statement, he must have been dwelling in a place beyond the mind, grounded in the unchanging soul of the universe, where reality isn't affected by duality. To him, hell didn't exist.

This is the treasure everyone is looking for, but where does one find it?

That's the great spiritual joke: it's never been lost. Spiritually, you are already perfect and have already attained what you are trying to find. Yet traditionally, this journey has been metaphorically described as the hero's *quest*. The seeker sets out from his home looking for treasure. He travels the seven seas, braves untold hardships, but fails at every turn. Finally, after a lifetime of searching, he returns home, broken in body and spirit, only to find the treasure buried under his own home. Similarly, the inner self, the drop of the ocean, the god within, has always been as close as a heartbeat, your constant companion. The veil obscuring the true self is so thin you don't recognize it, which is why when you finally do, you just might have to laugh at your own quest.

The search for the real self is the modus operandi of the Sufi dancers, the meditative runners, and the Zen masters with their seemingly crazy antics. A student might walk up and sincerely ask a Zen master a question and, without warning, the master might slap the student in the face. In one story, a teacher reportedly threw a student out a second-story window. These responses are not meant to be cruel or violent. They comprise a brilliant shock technique. In the instant of the slap or flying through the air, the mind is stunned out of habitual thought patterns, and in the lull, the student (hopefully) recognizes the real self.

If the Real Self Has Never Been Lost, Where Is It?

It's commonly said that the real self is buried like a hidden gem, a lotus under the mud. Some describe it as a mirror caked with dust—the mud and dust being the swirling chaos of the mind. But to say it's buried or hidden is energetically inaccurate. *Estranged* is a better term. We hear expressions such as "Someone's out to lunch," "I'm knocking on the door and no one's there," or "He's out somewhere in the ozone." It's becoming almost common to hear people frankly say, "I'm not in my body," and yet the movement of consciousness out of the body and its ramifications for health, peace, and clarity remain one of the least understood factors in health care and spirituality.

Finding the inner self may sound very New Age, but it's actually as old-school as it gets. Ancient cultures had a far better understanding of consciousness and what it meant to living than we do now. Thai culture believes there are thirty-two parts of the spirit located in various organs and parts of the body. Chinese medicine teaches that there are five parts of a person's spirit that reside in the organs. *Shen*, consciousness, is the spirit of the heart; *hun*, the ethereal soul, lives in the liver; *po*, the corporeal soul, resides in the lungs; *zhi*, or will, is located in the kidneys; and *yi*, the sprit of the spleen, is responsible for intellect.

A friend of mine who grew up in China once tripped over a curb as a child and fell into the street. Her grandmother took one look at her face and declared that her *shen* had been lost. She walked with the child to the exact spot of the accident, held her hand, and pleaded for her *shen* to return. Were these the ridiculous superstitions of an old woman? Indigenous peoples all over the world who have no contact with each other have similar beliefs.

Many indigenous peoples still insist that a human being's spirit belongs grounded in the body. If consciousness is disturbed, the chances of living a full life are much slimmer. Newborns are carefully evaluated to see if the spirit is intact and settled in the physical body. (You can see a shaman checking a newborn's spirit in Clint Eastwood's *Gran Torino*.) It's held that a person possesses only so much spirit and if it's not fully present, there's less of the real self available to live. In cases of birth or other trauma, it's believed that the inner essence may literally split or fragment off, be entangled in time, or go into another dimension. Unrooted babies are called shocked souls, and a healer/shaman is called to retrieve the lost part.

It may sound like an esoteric or primitive belief that has little to do with a modern person, but most of us have some degree of what the shamans call soul loss—in many cases, quite a large degree.

Science can't wrap around such concepts mainly because science is interested only in what can be seen and measured. If an object, or data from an object, can't be isolated, dissected, or quantified, it can't be studied. Your heart rate, how many pounds you weigh, the amount of cholesterol in your blood, a specific behavior—these can be measured. Consciousness cannot.

Nevertheless, the shaman, energy medicine therapist, and meditation master all use similar language to describe the fact that we aren't quite at home. Even psychology's concept of disassociation is ultimately the same: the real self isn't at home in the body.

But where is it? What is this world the shamans speak of, a place where it's possible to get stuck with another person, place, or time? There's nothing exotic or esoteric about it; they are simply referring to the mind. Mind, the valley of death, is a world of limitless nooks and crannies, formed and conditioned by concepts, belief systems, imagination, and trauma. The reason the real self has to be searched for in the first place is that the modern mind has become so reactive and dominant that it eclipses the real self to the point where we aren't aware that anything exists beyond it. That's the colossal joke of life: we think the mind, a mere instrument, is who we are. The mind has mutated into a dictator and the real self has been cast out.

A Zen saying goes, "Mind is hell, and no mind is heaven." The crucial point to grasp is that identifying with the mind is not conducive to bliss, peace, and stillness—these are the attributes of the inner self.

Powerful thoughts possess high-amplitude waves that jolt the nervous system and make it so that the inner self—consciousness—isn't comfortable in the body. The outward movement of consciousness happens so quickly one doesn't recognize moving out of the body at all. The cycle of leaving the body as a reaction to powerfully charged thoughts becomes chronic. The inner self becomes a stranger, hovering over one's shoulder. This isn't astral projection or anything like it. When one is enmeshed in the mind, consciousness is overshadowed and seems to disappear. The movement of consciousness is so subtle that it takes practice to learn what being out of the body actually means.

What Does the Inner Self Have to Do with Living Fully?

The real self is the still, clear presence that allows you be in the now. When this immortal part of you settles in your physical body, the timeless joins with the temporal. You experience the alchemy of the ancients, the marriage of yin/yang. To find the part that doesn't change is to find the drop within the ocean. When you know the drop, you'd better know the ocean.

Your mystic eyes begin to open, and the lines between you and life dissipate. You see the overall life force (love) in every living thing, and life becomes more alive and fresh. Take, for example, Vincent van Gogh's paintings. Clearly, he saw life differently from the average person; his paintings depicted a world bursting and swirling with energy.

You don't have to *try* to live fully; life is always available. You just have to be present to receive it. If the motor area of the brain were cut out, no one would be surprised that you couldn't walk. Likewise, if consciousness—the receptive faculty—isn't rooted in the physical body, you won't be able to fully receive life. Profound wonders continually pour from life, but if you're occupied in the mind, you'll miss it.

Say a man walks into his house and his dog jumps off the couch and runs over to greet him. The man is stressed and tired with a thousand racing thoughts. He pats the dog on the way to the refrigerator, grabs a beer, and looks at e-mails and surfs the web till dinner. After eating he watches TV—occupying himself—until it's time for bed. The next morning he goes to work and repeats the cycle.

The man missed the overwhelming joy in the dog's being as it ran over to him, its entire body wagging in happiness. He failed to receive the love in the dog's eyes, more real than any lover's. If he'd been present in the now, he would've been delighted, as he left for work, that the air was cool and fresh, dozens of roses scented the breeze, and droplets of water rested on the leaves. He might have felt the life force of the maple, seen that each tree and bush was bursting with aliveness, and noticed the breath of the wind flapping the leaves. He probably would've felt tremendous joy and gratitude. When one's inner self is at home, you receive from life—depression and boredom can't exist. You are so full that gratitude bubbles constantly from your heart. I call this "living elegantly": having awareness of the mutual interdependence of life and respect for the life force present in all living things.

To live elegantly is to go below the surface and see deeper into life. Take, for example, eating. Many approach food much like putting gas and oil into a machine. Conversely, to eat elegantly is to see every hand that helped to bring the food to your table: the farmer, the middleman, the trucker, and the grocer. Going deeper, you see nature: the seed, the sun, rain, earth, compost—and especially the sacrifice. Be it animal or vegetable, life is sacrificed so you can live another day.

In the Himalayas, many hunt the rare and valuable herbs that grow in the valleys. Legend has it that the precious herbs would show themselves only to one who had a pure heart and who would use them for noble purposes. The spirit of the herb came to the medicine woman while she slept and told her exactly where to find it, but the herbs would hide their faces from those who sought them for monetary gain. After gathering the plants, the medicine woman meditated over them to discern how best to prepare them for her patient. She prepared the plants with love, and when all was ready, she offered them to the sick individual. When one ingested herbs prepared elegantly, the results were reported to be miraculous. Today, when most herbs are grown commercially and slapped together in a factory, the benefit comes only from the medicinal chemicals present in the plants. Like the medicine woman's healing hand, it is the presence of our inner selves that allows us to live elegantly, going deeper into life.

Missing Life

The greatest regret of living is to miss life. Children grow, passing through the precious stages, but many parents miss much of it. Seasons come and go endlessly, bringing countless flowers, colors, and luxuriant new life, but because some people fail to see them—to *fully see*—the flowers don't really bloom for them. Most people remember only the especially good or bad things because they make a deep enough impression to jerk them into receptivity.

We go through life engrossed, like tourists taking pictures to capture every aspect of the trip. But people occupied in picture-taking miss the actual experience. When they get back home and look at the pictures, it's as if they were never there. Their pictures are a poor replacement for having the reality of life burned onto the tablets of their hearts and souls. For the same reason—because we miss so much of our lives—some people cry for humanity and some people laugh. Only what we're conscious of, what we're present for, makes an impression. The rest is a dream.

Without the Inner Self, You're Half Dead

My young children go rock-hunting and ooh and ah over common stones as if they were the most beautiful gems. It's a confirmed medical phenomenon that as we age, colors, tastes, and smells become less sharp, bright, and enjoyable. At what point does that happen? When does the enthusiasm and freshness of youth fade? How does the wonder of childhood get replaced with dissatisfaction, boredom, and stuckness? How do we become old in spirit? It's not physical age. It's a shift of consciousness from perceiving life as our receptive, innocent selves to interpreting life through the rose-colored glasses of our minds. Life is never boring; it's only the tedious well-worn ruts of the mind that make it so.

When the mind eclipses the still, clear, flowing place inside, it's like blinders blocking our inner vision. We become prisoners, limited by our own narrow viewpoint. The more mentally set in their ways people are, the more rigid and crotchety they become and the less wonder they possess. As time passes, their own minds can become a cage—and finally a hellish casket—because the eternal child, to whom life is a mystery, slowly withers and dies, and with it goes the aliveness and wonder of life. Estranging the child—the pure bright flame of consciousness—is the process of sickness, depression, decay, and death.

Once, my five-year-old daughter was invited to her friend's pool party. At the party, my ten-year-old, who had absolutely loved these parties just a few years ago, said with a trace of sadness, "Wow, this isn't as fun as it used to be." At ten, the ego mind is rapidly solidifying, and wonder is already well on its way to disappearing.

Christ supposedly said that to enter His father's kingdom, one must become again as a child. Becoming a child has also been the goal of Taoism and many paths, but how does one achieve this? First, one must find the child. (Not the inner child of psychology but the inner being, one's primal innocence, the clean slate.) The instant you recognize the real self, you discover that you aren't your mind or body at all but a vibrantly alive spark of consciousness. Even if you recognize your real self for only a fleeting instant, you'll find you enjoy life at a new depth. Later, you go beyond, the river enters the sea, and you see that you are the very substance of life.

Suggestions for Practice

The Part That Doesn't Change

I've interviewed hundreds of people over the age of eighty, many near death. The conversation often goes something like this:

"How are you feeling?"

"Okay, I guess. I'm old!"

"Do you feel old inside?"

Then comes a pause, a smile, or a laugh.

"Now that's the funny thing," they say, "because inside I'm young as ever. It's just this old body that's wearing out.

When I look in the mirror, I can't believe this long-toothed old biddy is staring back at me."

Ninety-nine out of a hundred people I've spoken with have said something similar. But the part of us that doesn't age is the witness, our inner consciousness, the part that doesn't change.

Can you find your inner consciousness? Better yet, can you get to know it?

Sit in a Dark Room

I mean so dark that you can't see anything at all, even after your eyes get used to it. As you sit in the total darkness, allow yourself to feel an inner aliveness. As you become absorbed in the sensations, the thoughts may slow and even cease. In that instant, when the thoughts stop, what's watching? Consciousness—the place that always knows bliss and peace. If there's space to walk around, try to experience yourself as consciousness just floating and moving through the air.

Between the Breath

Buddha reportedly taught a meditation where one focuses on the intervals between the breaths, and there's a sound reason for this technique. When we stop breathing, the mind also slows or even stops. Focusing on the space between breaths is really a lovely way to meditate. As you sit with your spine straight, pay attention to when the breaths stop. Don't force the intervals; just let your breathing be natural. In the space between the breaths, especially the out breath, you will have the opportunity to meet the witness.

Neti-neti

Since the inner self can't be adequately described by language, Vendanta, a school of Hindu philosophy, approaches discovering the true being by omission. *Neti-neti* is roughly defined as "not this, not this." The constant question you hold in your heart is "What am I?" As you approach life, you inquire and negate. If you look deeply, you see that your body is not you. You are not your mind, nor are you your pain and emotions. As you practice sincerely, you go deeper and deeper, negating all that you are not, and what remains is consciousness, the true self.

Nature Training

Immediately after taking care of your bathroom needs, go outside—preferably barefoot, on the grass, earth, or sand, in just about any weather—and watch the life around you.

It doesn't matter what nature is doing: sleeping, decaying, or bursting into life. As I write this, the clematis is blooming riotously, petals of the Daphne have fallen like pink snow, and the cherry is in full bloom. A hummingbird is watching me. She's perched on a tiny high branch of the plum. She buzzes off in a shower of white petals. Drops of water dot the strawberry plants, which are starting to perk up after their winter sleep.

There is a distinct flavor not only to every season but within each season, which may be split into young, middle, and old. Young spring sees the dormant coming to life and the first bloom. Middle or full spring is a riot of new growth. Old spring sees the blossoms dropping off and turns into young summer. There's always something new.

Nature captivates the mind. We can lose ourselves in nature, which is why Taoists and meditators of all backgrounds use nature as an ally. For example, imagine you're coming home from work and you see a huge hawk sitting on the fence. You're so absorbed in the hawk that your mind stops. If you're not thinking, what part of you is watching? Pure consciousness.

The problem is that the mind clicks in and takes over so quickly and powerfully that you miss the fact that, for a few seconds, your receptive part was at home in your body; you were in "no mind," experiencing life in absolute peace and stillness.

By becoming aware of the silence and the freedom that "no mind" brings, it is easier to notice when you've lost your freedom. Nature training makes it clear: The more intensely one is centered in the ego mind, the more anxiety one will have.

The more one lets go of the mind and blends with nature, the more peace and beauty one feels. It's not that one drops the mind—that's the negative approach. It's more that consciousness perceives itself, settles in the body, and replaces the mind as boss.

Dance

Sufi masters had their disciples dance furiously, sometimes for long periods of time. The dancer would be so moved by the music and involved in the movement that the mind dropped. At a signal, the dancer would abruptly stop. During the interval when one stopped movement, one could wake up to the true self.

Practice Staying in Your Body

Shamans perform soul retrievals, calling back the part of a person that's been lost, entangled, or stuck. After you recognize the difference between being in and out of your body, see if you can keep your clear consciousness grounded inside. Fear, anxiety, strong thoughts, daydreams—anything that keeps you in the mind estranges the presence of consciousness. You'll need to call your receptive self back into your body again and again. When you lose awareness, don't beat yourself up; just bring consciousness back again, and again.

Discipline is the constant practice, and discipline means awareness, awareness, and more awareness.

Staying in your body is not figurative or metaphorical. It's the practice of inner energetics, a shift of attention from the ego mind to the inner being. It's not difficult or complicated. When the mind is calm and still, consciousness settles naturally in the body. It's just that the mind has become such an overbearing dictator that we're hardly in the body at all. In the beginning, it may take a literal strengthening of your inner muscles so you can stay in the body and experience what's inside. As the part that doesn't change spends more time in the body, you understand what keeping consciousness in the forefront means. Life takes on different dimensions.

PART 3

The Fall from Grace
(How the Mind Became Master)

Chapter 6

Banished from the Garden of Eden

THE CONCEPT OF ORIGINAL SIN HAS BURDENED MILLIONS with a diabolic guilt trip, but original sin has nothing to do with sex, lust, morality, an inborn tendency toward sin, collective guilt, or the traditional definition of good and evil. The story of Adam and Eve represents the degradation of the undifferentiated one into duality. Eating the forbidden fruit from the tree of knowledge represents the loss of our spiritual selves. When one consumes knowledge, one automatically slips into the mental world of wrong and right.

Chinese cosmetology describes the same phenomenon without bringing the concept of sin into the equation. God, the whole of life or oneness, is depicted as a circle. They call it *yuan qi* or *wu qi*, the undifferentiated primal energy. When it moves, it becomes Liang I—positive and negative. When the two polarities interact, they become yin/yang. This is the phenomenon of the movement from wholeness to duality, from stillness to motion. When the one moves, it's degraded into two, and from the two, all things in life are born.

The only "sin" is that we've forgotten we are one with life and, instead, we identify with the mind. Our only fall from grace is believing we are separate entities.

The E.F. Hutton Phenomenon

If you go deeply enough into your mind, you will find nothing real or substantial. But at the onset of the journey, we think the mind/body is who we are. We wake up in the morning absolutely convinced that the voice in our heads (the separate self) is the voice of truth and reason. We trust and follow our mind like the Pied Piper, not realizing the great charge it has over us or how fully it programs us. We pay attention to its every whisper. I call this the E.F. Hutton phenomenon.

You must have seen the television commercial: A group of influential people sits around a large table in a busy restaurant. At other tables around them are hundreds of well-dressed, beautiful, apparently intelligent people. At the main table, the conversation turns to commodities, and someone asks a question. When a confident, attractive man starts to answer in a low voice, the entire restaurant goes into dead silence. Everyone, including the waiters, the bus boys, and the maître d', freezes on the spot. Ears strain to catch a tidbit of this authority's knowledge. When he stops speaking, everything slowly returns to normal. Small talk and movement return. The punch line is: "When E. F. Hutton talks, people listen."

It's an effective commercial, but the E.F. Hutton phenomenon is also exactly what has happened to us. When the voice in our head speaks, we listen! Typically, we regard our thoughts as creditable and reliable. We're completely enchanted, helpless in the clutches of our brain waves, especially the more powerful subconscious and unconscious ones. We take ourselves so seriously, but the voice of truth is merely the sum total of the events that have formulated our lives.

That's why people always think they're right. Of course they're right—from their point of view. Our entire lives prove our own viewpoints to be correct. Therefore, when we have a difference of opinion, we know the other party is misguided. But though we'll defend our beliefs and opinions— sometimes with our lives—every opinion is no more than a fart in the wind. It may be innocuous or it may stink, but if it comes from the ego mind, how much weight can it possibly carry? If a person is raised in a family of thieves and murderers, perhaps he believes it's honorable to kill and steal. Each of us implicitly believes the voice in our head, our personal E.F. Hutton. The ego mind has become as solid as a brick wall.

Ego Is a Quarrelsome Citizen

The ego has been called the reactive mind because ego often reacts powerfully when someone goes against what it thinks is right. Ego does not evolve much after childhood. In fact, as the years pass, ego frequently becomes more subtle, set in its ways, and troublesome. Young boys might fight over whose father is the best. As they get older, it becomes whose country, religion, or god is best. Every compassionate being wonders why we must hate. Why must we hurt each other? When ego's tail is stepped on, it must retaliate. Politicians' egos are responsible for wars and mass killing.

The Ego Mind's Nature Is to Fight and Toil

The ego struggles in three major areas: fighting with others, fighting with ourselves, and fighting with life itself.

Fighting with others is an energetic butting of heads, and I mean this literally. When you judge or disapprove of another, even if you speak no words, you assault them with negative mental/emotional energy. Mental/emotional warfare damages relationships and leaves both parties wounded. Fighting with ourselves is even more common than fighting with others. Turning ego's judgment upon ourselves creates an inner civil war. When we fight with life, we don't accept what life has given us. Ultimately, that resistance means swimming against the current or refusing to take the very medicine that will cure our disease.

If you toil and struggle in any of these three areas, it's a guarantee that anxiety and inner tension will follow. Fighting takes you from clear consciousness and right into the toil of the ego mind. If you find yourself toiling, you have certainly fallen from grace.

The Ego Is Only a Fish Story

If you want to live in peace and joy, return to the garden of ecstasy (oneness with life). To do so, you must lose confidence in the ego mind's authority. You have to fire it as your trusted adviser and get to the point where you regard what goes on in your mind as no more than a fish story.

Two men, now in their seventies, were lifelong fishing buddies. While still boys, one had a wild battle with a large trout that snapped the line and escaped before it reached the net. Neither saw the fish, but they knew it was huge because of its strength. Over the next six decades, the story slowly changed. It went from the fish breaking the line to the boy fisherman pulling a huge trout out of the water only to have it escape when he tried to net it. Eventually, the story morphed to fully catching the fish, which grew larger every few years. The man who hooked the fish has told the story so many times he firmly holds that it's truth. It's become part of his belief system. Likewise, his friend has heard the story so many times that it doesn't cause a ripple. Only in rare moments does he even remember: they never even saw a fish. That's what the ego is: a gigantic fish story. Although it's a dream, you implicitly believe in it.

To become a child again is to unlearn your fish story. If you went to one of the ancient mystery schools saying you wanted to learn, the teacher would throw you right out the door. Those schools are not places to learn but rather places to unlearn all the layers of brainwashing that have corrupted one's true nature. You must penetrate all the layers of falseness until you are naked, thereby regaining your primal innocence. But this entails walking through all the dead material of your mind until your inner self clearly sees your story for what it is. You, as an ego mind, aren't as real as you may believe. What you think you are is merely a chain of events and memories.

How We Fell from Grace (The Creation of a Fish Story)

It's said that a child is born a blank sheet of paper, clean and fresh, but that's only partially true. Even if we dismiss latent impressions from past lives or why we were attracted to our parents in the first place, our education begins well before birth. During our time in the womb, we perceive every emotion of the mother via the umbilical cord. Dad is felt through the mother's reaction when she sees or thinks about him.

Unlike popular beliefs, the womb may not be a perfect, sheltered, utopian place of peace. During the pre- and perinatal stages is when many of our deepest wounds originate. In fact, the womb is often where we first learn how to leave the body. It may be the only recourse we have to protect ourselves.

After nine months of internalizing the mother's emotions, an infant comes out into the world. The pre-verbal newborn still operates mainly on feeling and sensing, yet she's remarkably receptive. She sees and feels energetic exchanges between people and takes in parental vibrations like a sponge. Deep in her consciousness, she is already learning what a man and a woman are and how they should act. It's the child's unbelievable receptiveness that makes the brainwashing process so rapid and effective. Children see and hear everything, and they mold to it.

Innocence Lost

Look at the eyes of young children. Without a firmly crystallized sense of self, young kids still possess innocence. They stand with a full belly sticking out, food all over their faces—blissfully ignorant. A young kid doesn't care what people think about his or her appearance and has yet to learn shame. But any parent can observe how innocence fades like an ephemeral flame.

The murder of a child's innocence should be studied and kept in mind always, because the secret of living fully is reversing the process. Look at a tree. Feel the energy of it; it's just being, flowing without obstruction. It has no mind to crimp the flow of life. A dog is also flowing, but it has a mind, granted a far less complicated one than humans have. But a dog is sometimes bothered, which may temporarily cloud its flowing. A young child is flowing, much more than an adult, until the corruption begins—and it begins quickly.

We as a society have been schooled with a negative system. Children are naturally exuberant, happy, and bubbling with joyous energy. But when the child expresses it, the parents nip it in the bud. If children run around like crazy making noise, they're told to settle down and be quiet. Heaven forbid they touch their private parts. Children are uninhibited nudists until they're shamed into wearing clothes. I grieved when my five-year-old son became ashamed—his baby-sitter taught him it was shameful—to be seen naked. Many parents had the joy trained out of them, and they train it out of their children with the same fear and guilt trips. They take fresh, joyously alive children and make them as sick and stressed out as adults, using the same fear tactics as a brainwasher. They give praise, love, and acceptance if a child does what they deem correct and withdraw it when a child doesn't live up to their ideal or goes against the grain. But who says the parental standard is correct? The parents' viewpoint is simply a byproduct of their own brainwashing.

More and more parents are refusing to hit their kids, but discipline through guilt, shame, and condemnation is merely a subtler form of violence. When a child is five years old, psychology says, the majority of her personality has already been formed. In other words, primal innocence is already well on the way to being corrupted.

Puberty: The Crystallization of Self

The advent of puberty is more than hormones going wild. The child comes into her own identity. Now she scrutinizes herself in the mirror as if for the first time—a new and frightening world. When our neighbor's child turned thirteen, she stared at her body and face every time she passed a reflective surface. A few zits on the face were the end of the world. With puberty, the idea of "me" becomes far stronger—maddening even. The child's ego is now firmly crystallized into an identity. As the years pass, the bars of the cage become stronger and more solid.

Suggestions for Practice

What's Your Fish Story?

Is your fish story that you are a thirty-nine-year-old American female who works as an Internet marketer, with a husband and two children? Is it that you are a liberal Democrat and Buddhist who is allergic to wheat and dairy? If you had no fish story, who and what would you be? Another way to put this is, what were you before your story began?

Where Are You Toiling?

The entire method of practice is to go deeper and deeper into your mind and to observe what is causing you to lose clarity and the presence of the real self. When you descend into the ego mind, that's a guarantee you've lost clear consciousness and are not grounded in the body. Look over your life and observe when and where your ego is fighting. Are you fighting with others, with yourself, or against life itself?

Chapter 7

Splitting the Mind with Fear, Greed, and Guilt

Since the beginning of time, leaders and shepherds of men have masterfully controlled the masses by controlling their minds. It's the conqueror's credo: united you stand, divided you fall. *Divided*, in this case, means to stay centered in the ego mind, away from your real self. People centered in their real selves are threatening to those in power. Those who live life from their true selves are independent and powerful. They are already free and don't need to be led. Free people, by their very presence, shake up the system. Political and religious leaders prefer drugged sheep that are weak and easy to control.

To keep the masses fixed in the ego mind, rulers universally employ desire, fear, greed, and guilt. Fear, of course, is the strongest weapon for knocking people off balance and controlling them. Every marketer knows it's more influential to speak to people's fear than even their greatest desires. If I'm selling a DVD on yoga and advertise that it will bring better health, some may buy it. However, if I suggest that it will prevent cancer or heart disease, many more will take notice. Fear touches a raw nerve, and those who work in the arena of power—priests, politicians, and those who want your money—know how to use fear to keep you fragmented.

It's easy to keep one centered in the ego mind, because we already believe in our separateness. In the seventies the book *A Course in Miracles* came out. The Course was, and still is, influential because it was embraced by prominent leaders who in turn spread its message to millions. A major tenet of *A Course in Miracles* is that there are only two emotions—love and fear—and that fear arises when we are separate from God.

That sentence should be deeply meditated upon because it must have been uttered by someone who profoundly experienced oneness with life.

Centered in the ego mind—our little egg—we're split off, fragmented, separate from the whole. We don't remember our real selves, and the garden of ecstasy is just a misty dream. We don't understand where our longing for fulfillment comes from, why we have nebulous fears, or how to make things right. The world is seen and experienced in relation to "ourselves" and "our lives." Naturally, we become self-centered and fearful. We're compelled to compare ourselves to others. Ego would like to be a cut above its neighbor and must compete to do so. Ego wants to be special, but its secret fear is that it is unlovable and not good enough. This is the diabolical Catch-22 of the ego: it longs to be special and cherished, but by the very fact of its separateness, the ego knows it's lacking, which is why we can't truly love our ego selves. Being separate makes us susceptible to being split further and intensified even more into the ego. Let's look at the ways in which this happens.

Fear, Greed, and Guilt

Religion's message is clear: follow the laws, obey the rules, and life will smile on you. Health, love, and financial prosperity will be yours. (The most brilliant religionists clearly relate the spiritual to the material.) When this life is over, you'll go to heaven, where all your needs will be met forever—appealing to an obvious mental greed. If you don't live up to the standard, there's eternal damnation—you'll go to hell, the ultimate punishment. If you prefer the good karma/bad karma model, the message is that if you are a good person, you'll receive good in return. Do bad and it will catch up to you.

It's your own consciousness that creates your life and karma, not your actions. While you can do "good" on the outside, your inner heart may not be true. Doing "good" out of desire to go to heaven, or out of fear of hell, or because of guilt or shame, will do no good at all. Being kind for a reward is ugly, and faking that your heart is in the right place is downright false. There is no merit in falseness. It's a big zero. Awakening is not a concept or a philosophy; it has to be real.

You may perform ten thousand prostrations, but unless your true heart enters into the movements, they are worthless—except perhaps for the physical exercise they provide. You may pray constantly, have the word of God in your mind, or chant the most sacred mantra with little or no merit. Doing nothing with a sincere heart is far better than the grandest ceremony without sincerity. On the spiritual path, you can't "fake it till you make it."

Some say that when we die, God judges us. Others say an angel or the king of the dead judges us. But it's not that you are judged. You simply can't hide what you are—not ever. The truth of your inner heart can never be concealed. Life can't be fooled, and you don't have to wait until you die to reap your so-called karma. What's in your heart is reflected to you now and always. Your consciousness creates your life on the inside and out. Heaven or hell is self-created.

Nevertheless, religion's fear tactics work. Many people are too lazy to go inside and find truth; they'd rather be spoon-fed what to believe. Religion gives the mind something to bite into; there's a clear path to follow, a standard of excellence to live up to. The fear and the guilt trip are extraordinarily clever and very hard to shake. Most of us have had it bred so deeply into us that we try to follow the rules—just in case. If it is true, we'd better keep all bases covered. If you think about it from a motivational or marketing viewpoint, it's brilliant.

The Truth about Morals and Ethics

Laws are mental constructs, so naturally they keep you stuck in the mind where there is a clear delineation between right and wrong and good and evil. Laws won't set you free—they will probably cause you greater inner conflict, thereby enslaving you to a greater degree. Never forget: if you are in the mind, you have already fallen from grace (unity).

Most spiritual paths insist that one must lead a "good" life, implying that one should be honest, chaste, and pure. The rationale is that when you follow a moral and ethical code, it will pave the way to growth and awakening, much like good soil provides ideal conditions for crops. It seems plausible enough, but having a code to live by is merely a substitute for the awareness and true spontaneity that come with awakening. Moral and ethical systems contain generalized truths that make sense to those who aren't willing to go inside and find real truth.

A Cookbook Approach

If you want to find out which foods are causing inflammation in your body, you could perform an elimination diet, a laborious process that can take many weeks. During the clean-out phase, you'd omit most common reaction-causing foods, such as dairy, wheat, soy, corn, tomatoes, and so on. Then, in a long reintroduction or testing phase, you'd go back to eating your favorite foods to see exactly which cause symptoms of inflammation. By the time you complete the process, you'll have a good idea of your optimal diet. For those unwilling to go through the full procedure, I might suggest a cookbook approach: giving up wheat, sugar, and all pasteurized dairy without testing anything. Most people will get significant results simply by giving up these three common sensitivity-triggering foods.

Religious laws appear to operate in the same vein: they address the most common sticky spots. If you can navigate through the trouble areas, you might alleviate mental "inflammation." If your mind and body are more peaceful, you might get closer to the place of surrender. Trouble is, these laws rarely work. Life is too big to be put in such small boxes.

For example, the Ten Commandments are a collection of laws that provide a detailed, predetermined code for how to live your life. They tell you exactly what you should do (worship only one God, honor your parents, and keep the

Sabbath) and also exactly what you should not do (commit murder or adultery, steal, lie, and so on). If you memorize the Ten Commandments, you will have a preset answer to some of life's biggest questions. When situations arise, you might have a good idea what to do. If you do the right thing in any given situation, you'll be considered a morally correct individual. You might be proud of that designation and hope to be recognized or perhaps even rewarded for it. (Note that pride for doing the "right" thing is a subtle development of the ego.)

But is it possible that there are exceptions to these laws? For example, might there be good lies?

One of my patients told me about an incident that happened thirty years before. Sometimes, when her husband came home drunk, he'd beat their young son. For some reason, he made the boy the sole target of his abuse, physically harming no one else. One day, the boy broke the window with his baseball. That evening the husband came home drunk, noticed the window, and said, "Who the hell did this?" His wife looked at him and, without batting an eye, said "I did."

That was a good lie.

Had the woman been yoked to the moral precepts of the Ten Commandments, she would have been compelled to tell the truth and her son would have suffered.

How about adultery? *The Bridges of Madison County*, a novel made into a classic movie, tells the story of a married woman, Francesca (Meryl Streep), who has a torrid love affair with a visiting photographer (Clint Eastwood). In the story, if Francesca hadn't broken the rules, she never would have known how far she could open her heart. She never would have experienced the kind of love few are lucky enough to know. That might be called a good adultery, or certainly a necessary one to Francesca's life.

And though I don't wish harm to anyone, one might even argue that there are good murders. Everything has its place. Awakened people don't need laws or recipe books to tell them what to do in any given moment. They just have to be aware enough to know what to do, and when. Laws, rules, and ideals, more often than not, cause greater mental inflammation.

Laws Keep You Mired in the Mind

When you join a club or another organization, there will always be rules. If you don't follow them, you simply won't belong. Going against the grain casts doubt and shakes up others' faith. In nature, birds of a feather flock together. Similarly, people flock together to share common habits and belief systems. Sharing beliefs is comforting as well as confining. For example, in a group of wine tasters, one can expect that everyone will drink wine. But if one goes against the expected code of a group, sooner or later that person becomes an outcast. This is especially true when it comes to established religious paths, because when religion is brought into the mix, the rules of good and evil are even more tightly defined and scrutinized. However, we might say that every spiritual master in history was a rebel who turned the status quo upside down. But when each master died, followers formed a new status quo and created a new club around that master's teachings.

Exactly what dynamic does having rules establish? Obviously, a strictly defined right and wrong. Expectations are created around the rules. If you live up to those expectations, you are considered good. If you slip from the standard of so-called excellence, you become less than good—a sinner. Such judgments can create severe psychological conflict because good and bad parts of you are subsequently defined and you can never be good enough.

What does it mean to be thought of as good? Good in what sense, or by whose standard? That depends on what model and whose morals and ethics you've adopted. But it's a sure bet that following any standard of perfection to become an upright, righteous person will get you stuck as if you were in quicksand. Such ideals weren't made to help you be a better person; they were made to control you so you fit into society at large.

If people believe that killing, stealing, or having sex with the neighbor's wife will prevent God from smiling and thus close the doors of prosperity, they tend to think twice. Precautionary beliefs are strong deterrents that prevent havoc in the streets. But our minds have been cluttered with laws; they're embedded in our consciousness. They don't bring real freedom; they keep us enslaved in fear.

Read about the lives of the saints—of any religion. They're tortured over the ideals that religion has set down. A monk sits in his cell going through an inner battle. He's celibate because he was told that abstaining from sex is a higher path. He's managed to control his body, but he still has desire, and thinking of sin is the same as sin. So he struggles and frets about a natural, pleasurable part of life. He doesn't transcend desire. It's repressed until he becomes a quivering mess, especially if he finds someone desirable. This type of inner battle pits your willpower against your natural urges. But in a civil war there are no winners.

Self-denial and repression do not bring enlightenment. They facilitate not growth but only unnecessary torture. Many people gravitate toward this inner struggle because they secretly love to torture themselves. In religion, suffering is glorified; the best saint is always the one who has gone through the most hardship and denied himself the most. No standard of perfection, however, can set you free. Trying to be perfect is a head-centered path, a way to keep score that's guaranteed to develop the ego and keep you perpetually stuck.

Religion tells us that if you love God enough and live correctly, He will show himself to you. But again, if you read the lives of the saints, this is one of the most common ordeals.

No matter what the seeker does, God remains unseen. Even Mother Teresa said that although she believed in God, He seemed to have forsaken her. Perhaps you aspire to see spiritual masters in your inner vision and travel to higher planes, yet you close your eyes and don't see anyone or go anywhere. You read about great miracles and the powers the saints have, and although you try to be as sincere and disciplined as anyone, you never have such grand experiences. What are you doing wrong? Your mind might tell you you'd better try harder to be purer and more righteous. So ensues a war between your "good" and "bad" selves, which only keeps you in perpetual chaos, cemented in the mind.

Easy to Become Fanatic

On one side are the so-called sinners, those who don't follow the rules. When the pendulum shifts, you have the fanatics who follow the rules to the letter—and the fanatics are in far worse shape than the sinners. Religious fanatics are usually very sick people, internally tied up in knots.

A simple life is good for inner growth because the more you simplify, the less you have to think and worry about. It's easier to turn your attention inside. But does this mean it's better to deny yourself every pleasure? When one becomes a fanatic, it has the opposite effect. To illustrate this point, I like to think of an old martial arts story.

A young student talks with his teacher: "Martial arts is everything to me. I want to follow in your footsteps and become a master."

"Okay," the teacher says. "But I warn you, it takes years of committed practice."

"How long will it take?"

"If you're sincere and work hard, about twenty years."

"What if I practice every day, ten hours a day? What if I work twice as hard as everyone else—then how long will it take?"

The master thought a moment and replied, "Forty years."

"Forty years! I'll work harder than anyone you've ever seen. I'll—"

"Maybe never," the teacher said.

Buddha created his famous middle path after experiencing the extreme ways of the ascetics. Discipline, Buddha realized, was useful, but starving and mortifying the body to find the spirit was just plain stupid. Harming the physical body only kept one centered in the body/mind, which made awakening impossible. When Buddha broke from the group, the ascetics defiled his name, chastised him for weak character, and labeled him a deserter—a typical response when one breaks the rules of the group.

Monasteries Are for the Unawakened

Many people assume that monks and nuns are more peaceful, joyous, and spiritually advanced than the layperson.

However, that assumption often doesn't hold true. Many gravitate to the monastery because it provides a safe, sheltered life. One doesn't have to deal with making a living, paying the bills, cultivating intimate relationships, or raising a family. The times I've spent in ashrams and monasteries seemed to validate this point. Some of the residents bickered among each other, quarreling like alley cats. The majority seemed to me unawakened people with personal problems who'd found a place to hide from the pressures of society. In India, where so many hold themselves up as enlightened men and women, it's believed that fewer than 10 percent of them are genuine. The rest have found a safe niche or a platform for making a living.

It's been said that a pirate has a better chance to awaken than a monk. World-renowned author Jack London might agree. In London's autobiographical novel *John Barleycorn*, he described how he became an alcoholic. As a young writer, London knew that to write interesting and exciting stories, he had to find people who lived larger than life. He didn't find them in the monasteries. To London's thinking, those in the temples lived desperate, boring lives not worth writing about. London found life's exciting characters in the taverns, watering holes, and brothels of the world. In getting to know these men and women, London did what they did, and in the process he developed a fondness for drink. Yet in the telling of his adventures and the exploits of those he associated with, London became one of the most beloved writers in history.

I'm not praising pirates or drunks, but rather suggesting that the courage necessary to take a chance can serve you on both the inner and outer path. I'm also not implying that genuine saints don't exist within religious systems, but I submit that their awakening happened despite laws, not because of them. Awakening is letting go of control and going beyond the ego mind, which is limited by the duality of right and wrong.

Awakening: The Birth of True Morals

Morality doesn't breed awakening; that's backward. Awakening breeds morals—genuine morals. If there's any universal law, it's "do no harm": do whatever you want, but don't hurt anyone else. But after you awaken, you don't have to think about it. You automatically make the "right" decision, which means making the best choice in the moment for everyone and everything concerned. You simply can't do otherwise.

Before awakening, Buddha was a young prince from India. He had a beautiful wife and the finest of everything. His father, the king, wanted his son to see only beauty and surrounded him with the most opulent splendor. He was shielded from the ugly, poor, sick, and aged. But one day the prince escaped from the watchful eye of his servants and strolled around the city. For the first time, he saw the sick, old, misshapen, and crippled.

The need to alleviate human pain consumed the prince. He abandoned his kingdom, determined to find truth, so he could help eradicate the suffering of sentient beings. Mohammed, Christ, Mahavir, and every one of the sages had similar experiences. But this compassion doesn't come from scriptures. You can't read about spirituality, grasp it intellectually, or memorize the proper way.

After you see that all life is one energy, your heart becomes full and tender. You won't want to hurt anything else, because you'll know that, ultimately, to do so hurts you. You'll understand exactly how Buddha arrived at compassion for every sentient being. You'll see why people followed Christ. Christ lived states of consciousness that others, even the learned priests of his time, never came close to experiencing. Christ's very being evoked ecstasy; he was drunk with love. He was in a place beyond the mind. When he said "follow me," and people took one look at his face and dropped everything to follow him. His teaching was pure love and little else.

With even the slightest touch of awakening, you'll get it. You'll love life so much you'll feel an overwhelming desire to eradicate suffering any way you can. Your motivation won't be from guilt, fear of retribution, or greed for reward. Your heart will simply become an overflowing river of love—the true development of the heart center. When kindness, compassion, and love are real, you don't need to try to be or do good. It's the only thing you can do.

Society Picks Up the Torch

You may think you've avoided the fear and the guilt trips of religion, but they can hardly be avoided, because religious values are firmly embedded in the consciousness of society. Society molded our grandparents and the teachers who taught our parents, right down the line to us.

Modern society appears to encourage free thinkers, but this is true only so far. It doesn't matter so much how outrageous someone is or the nature of a person's beliefs and philosophies or even how far one goes against the status quo. What matters is how influential one becomes. If one starts shaking the foundations of society or its established values, there will be repercussions. For example, when natural medicine started gaining popularity in the late eighties, a few medical doctors embraced drugless methods. Trouble was, they became a little too influential. When pioneer nutritionist Jonathan Wright, MD, openly battled the Food and Drug Administration, armed FDA agents stormed his office and placed him under arrest. His medical license was suspended for ninety days, and he was fined and put on probation. Society seeks to maintain fundamental values as they are. Those who follow the game are rewarded with wealth, honors, titles, and respect. Those who don't follow risk disgrace, or worse. Those who went against the Maoist regime in China, for instance, risked execution.

In older cultures the rules are simpler and more clearly defined. A man knows exactly what a man is supposed to be, and the rules of behavior for women are just as clear. Every role is mapped out: a child understands how to act, as does a parent, a grandparent, a rich man, a poor man, high caste, or low caste. From chief to slave, everyone knows his or her place. It's much harder to make a mistake in an older society, and there's a certain ease and comfort in staying within the fold of the expected, because then you're considered proper and correct and therefore a good person.

Most people are easily controlled by societal expectations. The ego loves fitting in and being applauded for doing the right thing, and that type of conditioning begins when we're quite young. My daughter came home from her second day of first grade with a gold star, awarded for showing responsibility (doing what was expected). She was pleased as punch and pursued earning more gold stars to try to reach the top tier of her class. When she reached that tier, she received an award and even greater recognition. Perhaps the longing for acceptance and recognition is why we gravitate toward groups or tribes of like-minded people, but there are rules and ideals for every group we join.

To this day in rural Thailand, the most cherished possession is for others to think of one as a good person. Everyone watches everyone else to uphold the ideal. People gossip a lot, so one can't go too far astray without someone noticing and spreading the word. If a girl has a boyfriend, everyone knows about it. If she goes out with another man, she's a tramp—not a good person. The system works to effectively control people to conform to established ideals. In America, if one wants to drink, drug, or whore himself to death, it's ridiculously easy. In rural Thai society, it's much harder to slip, with so many eyes watching. People are caught before they get too far, and they have their honor to worry about—and the honor of their entire families, including their ancestors. They must ask themselves: what will people think or say?

One of my patients, an Asian psychologist in her fifties, couldn't get past the ideal that had been hammered into her: a woman's happiness is permitted only after her husband and family are happy. It was even more deeply instilled because love had been used in the conditioning. Her father, whom she dearly loved and respected, genuinely believed in the Confucian way, a formative element of Asian society, and he'd taught her the ideal personally. She was a modern, intelligent woman—she understood that it was society's way of controlling and subjugating women—but it was too deeply embedded for her to fully break free of. It caused her great resentment and inner struggle.

Brainwashed before Twenty

By the junior year of high school, one is well-schooled in the consciousness of society, and even more so in its unconscious values. There are many layers of parental, religious, and societal conditioning that pull us so subtly that we're not even aware how much they influence us. By the time we're grown, we no longer need the parents, teacher, or priest. Their job has been done well. Their voices are imprinted in our minds; they've become our conscience. Now we fragment ourselves by upholding ideals that keep us in conflict. These voices contribute a great deal to our deep unconscious fish stories. They should be unlearned through careful observation.

Guilt and Fear—a Way of Life

We've become so accustomed to anxiety, fear, and guilt that our minds and bodies have molded to them. We consider it a positive to be stressed into action. Jack LaLanne suggested that people begin the journey toward better health by standing in front of a mirror and scrutinizing their figure, eyeballing just how far they'd let themselves go. He believed that guilt, disgust with one's self, and fear of the future were great motivators. It works from a marketing perspective, but while it may sell more product, it's a negative approach and thus counterproductive. Guilt defeats the purpose because anything that causes nervous tension is, ultimately, anti-health. These types of motivators may make you move, but they keep you isolated in the ego and take you away from your real self and awakening.

By Adulthood, the Cage of the Ego Is Completely Formed

As an adult with a fully crystallized ego, one tries to find happiness. In your own adulthood, you may have done everything you were supposed to do: find a spouse/partner, have children, get a good job, make a lot of money, join churches and temples, and have many friends and activities. Yet deep down you might still feel a vague anxiety, unhappiness, and the sense that there's more to life. Perhaps there comes a point of deep frustration and despair: the soul hungers for truth. So you look more deeply into religion, yoga, and philosophy, study with teachers of all kinds, and read countless books. But this is merely more brainwashing. More layers of ideals and concepts are piled on top of the already prodigious load. After a lifetime of collecting knowledge and concepts, you've built a grand edifice of an ego, but the innocent child is gone.

When Christ said to become like a child again, the word *again* was the key. Children are naturally innocent merely because they have yet to be corrupted. Becoming like a child again is to de-corrupt yourself from the massive load of crap in your mind. De-corruption happens when you see that you're wearing a thousand layers of other peoples' clothes and you start removing them until you're naked. Lao Tzu, the founder of Taoism, supposedly said: "When I was young I gathered unto myself something new every day. And when old, every day I let something go."

Suggestions for Practice

Begin with Compassion

Begin the journey inside by being nice. In order to even start to untie the great knot of the ego, you have to stop fighting with yourself. Get out of the concept of original sin, being right, good, and proper, and the other ideals that have been brainwashed into you. Throw out all comparisons between you and anyone else.

Simply bring in the light of clear consciousness and watch.

Live Your Own Code of Ethics

Where does your value system come from? How are fear, guilt, and greed keeping you fragmented? You don't have to think about it. Better to observe the many voices in your head: rights, wrongs, prejudice, insecurities, the no-saying voice, and all the others. You don't need to know where or who they came from; just watch with clear consciousness.

Get beyond others' laws of right and wrong. Better to find your own code of values, which can be done by going inside yourself and exploring the reasons you've become tangled up in the first place. You will see that, spiritually, you are already perfect. It's the ego mind that's all snarled up with laws, concepts, and expectations of what you should be. With observation, you can formulate your own code to live by simply by avoiding what causes you internal conflict. When you go against the code of your own soul, your heart will tell you something is wrong. (Understanding how to use your heart as a barometer to formulate your personal code is covered in more detail in Chapter 14.)

PART 4

Unlearning

Chapter 8

Not Therapy

To wade through all the crap is a challenge, and no one can do much for you—at least not in the deepest sense. Our distortions can't be taken away by another human being, be it doctor, healer, counselor, spiritual master, or shaman. That's why I insist that we can't truly heal ourselves with psychology, regression, affirmations, positive thinking, tapping acupuncture points (a method used in Thought Field Therapy and Emotional Freedom Technique), or the ample smorgasbord of other therapies. They are superficial bandages that don't treat the core. It's impossible to awaken with the mind, and it's not possible to heal the self by talking about it. The best anyone—or even the cleverest of therapies—can do for you is to inspire you to approach the edge of yourself, which may help, depending on to what degree you actually go inside. Only you, however, can walk through the valley of death to the core.

How can it be otherwise? If it were possible for someone to awaken *for* you, the spiritual path would be easy. Awakenings would be dime a dozen, and large numbers of humanity would be awake. But how can anyone become aware for you? How can anyone face your demons for you? No one can. The path inside—the inner work—must be navigated by the individual.

No matter what you wish to do in the world, you have got to walk the road yourself. If you want to be a skilled martial artist, you won't get anywhere by talking about it. You have to train for years, repeating the basic skills tens of thousands of times. And perfecting the moves is only the most rudimentary level. Then you have to use your tools, to make them work against others in practice and in competition. You can expect to be defeated and to eat humble pie many times. Even after many years of totally committed work, you find not just a few opponents with more skill but many. Practice continues. You hone and discard all superfluous movement until perhaps one day you become completely spontaneous, in a state of no mind.

Who else can walk this road for you? You might have the greatest teacher on the planet, but she can't do any more than guide you. She can't do one iota of the work for you. You have to go through every step of it yourself. Ultimately, martial arts, or anything worth having, becomes a road inside; everything follows the same inner path of facing the mind. It's never mattered what path one takes; they all lead to the same place. What matters is going in.

I read a story about a famous spiritual teacher who used to take a daily ritual bath in the Ganges River. The Ganges is thought to be a sacred river that has the power to wash away one's sins. One day, while the teacher was swimming, a ragged hermit showed up with a golden bowl filled with feces. He was sitting on the shore vigorously polishing the bowl. The teacher climbed out from the water and asked: "What on earth are you doing, man? No amount of polishing is going to make that bowl of crap presentable."

The hermit didn't bother to reply, and instantly the teacher became awakened. No matter how vigilantly one tries to work from the outside, it can't touch the shit inside.

Most therapies and self-help methods work from the outside trying to fix the ego, which has been molded by the events of our lives and the way we've been conditioned. Those things aren't real, though, because the formative element of ego comes not from actual events but from our perception and interpretation of them. Put fifty people in a room who witness exactly the same thing and ask them to describe what happened. The perceptions and interpretations will be so different that you'll hardly believe they were all in the same place. Perception and interpretation are not reality. They act as filters, cataracts on reality. The mind thinks it sees clearly, but the lens is clouded. Most of us don't see reality at all. We create our own separate worlds colored by fear, desire, and habit—a world that isn't real. To see reality, we have to remove the filters of judgment, prejudice, interpretation, and analysis and see through the eyes of the true self.

Since most people think they *are* their minds and bodies, it's through mind and body that they attempt to live a better life. Frankly, that doesn't work as well as they'd like. Ego-based cures will always be limited for the very reason that we're dealing with distortion.

Therapy is limited by illusion. One could even say that, much of the time, the therapist is in cahoots with the patient. The patient comes in with a personal issue, which, of course, is an ego problem, and the therapist tries to help—with the distorted perceptions and interpretations that the patient has provided.

For example, if I see a therapist because my girlfriend gets angry and hits me, I might get some practical advice, such as to leave her. If I choose to go deeper, we might look at my behaviors and beliefs and where they came from. We might explore past wounds and relationships with my family to see why I keep re-creating the problem. Of course, at this point, some official diagnosis will probably be tagged to my condition—such as neurosis, obsessive-compulsive disorder, depersonalization, bipolar disorder, or borderline personality disorder—which embeds the problem more firmly in my psyche. But on a deeper level, there is no problem. Actually, the ego is the problem, and, of course, the therapist has his own perceptions, interpretations, projections, and judgments that can get in the way.

Getting to the point of strong emotion doesn't cut it. The film *Good Will Hunting* highlights such a pivotal moment of healing. Hunting, an abused genius, has completely repressed and protected himself from feeling his childhood wounds. He is led, through caring therapy, to the point of re-experiencing his pain and sorrow. After a good cry, he gets over the hump. But such portrayals are misleading. A person can be stuck in emotions for years without resolving anything. Getting to the point of strong emotion may or may not be a first step. If one is unconscious and out of the body, emoting doesn't do much except relieve steam like the valve of a pressure cooker—and use a lot of tissues.

Finding the original cause of our problems is almost useless. Putting focus into a dream that has no substance only validates and cements the perceived problem more firmly. That's always been the danger with labeling: now the mind has something to chew up, a problem to ruminate on. The mind loves having a diagnosis. I've seen patients with obscure problems shop for a doctor until one finally figures out what label to pin on it. Though their problem didn't improve with the diagnosis, just having a name to call it gives one relief because it placates and occupies the mind.

From an ego point of view, self-love—the hallmark of New Age self-help psychology—is amusing. How can we have deep esteem for the part of us that's been unworthy and not good enough for our entire lives? How can we love the part we've invested a lifetime into making unlovable and unwanted? Parents, teachers, and religion have condemned us for being who we are, and we've unwittingly picked up the torch and kept condemning ourselves. We've been calling ourselves "fool," "idiot," and "moron" for decades. We've looked in the mirror and seen ugliness and shortcomings as far back as we can recall. How is it possible to suddenly love what we've criticized for so long?

No amount of cheerleading can make that shift. It would be far more honest to simply admit we have insecurities around our identity or even don't like ourselves and start from there, rather than continually pretending and carrying on. It's perfectly natural for the ego to feel small, unworthy, and less than—by the very nature of its separateness. When you meet your real self, you'll see that you literally *are* love. You are a veritable ray of sunshine. What a vast difference from trying to love yourself! When you know what you *really* are, there's no need to bolster self-love or self-esteem. Until then, the best way to "love yourself" is to take care of your body's needs and respect your true feelings.

Positive thinking is, in effect, a form of repression. How can positive thinking help to change deep-seated patterns? Dwarfing the power of the conscious mind is the vast unconscious. It's ludicrous to think that a few hopeful thoughts will eclipse the massive unconscious programming we're not even aware of.

Affirmations are also a wishy-washy attempt at keeping your mind positively programmed. There is a sense of desperation to these methods, and in the end we must admit they haven't worked as well as we'd hoped, again because the attempt to transplant positive programs into the mind can't overcome the deeper realities of the subconscious and unconscious mind. It's like trying to bail out a rowboat that has a huge gaping hole, or like the child with his finger in the dike trying to hold back the sea. No matter how frequently one tries to keep a positive affirmation or thought, one can't hold it forever. This is especially clear when we are faced with thoughts and circumstances that bring up fear. When one is activated into shock, all that self-hypnosis goes up in smoke. The mind's knee-jerk reaction to fear is the same as always.

It seems that much of the work in the field of affirmations is fear-based. We want financial abundance, so we set up a mantra for it. We want health, so we set up an intention. We want love and imagine a perfect partner. But underneath, our desire for abundance may actually stem from the fear of not having. Covering fear with a prayer or intention doesn't work. The fear is still the deeper program, and the law of reverse effort kicks in: that which we don't want may happen. The fear will attract more strongly than the weaker intention. To have clear intentions, one must get to the core.

The law of attraction—as outlined in books such as *The Secret* and *Think and Grow Rich*—is, in my opinion, misunderstood. The idea that what we hold in our mind will eventually manifest in the physical plane is only partially true.

In martial arts, everyone would like to be a Bruce Lee or an Anderson Silva, but very few actually become great. Asked if he's committed, a student may swear he'll do anything to improve, and on the outside he appears to be moving forward. Unconsciously, however, that may not be the case. Perhaps he's afraid, too uncomfortable to face himself, or just doesn't want it enough to go through all the challenges. So life dishes out roadblocks. He gets injured, has a family problem, or has a schedule change come up at work. Any one of a thousand perfectly understandable problems may arise that require immediate attention, thereby sabotaging his training.

It happens in every aspect of life. A lonely man insists he'd give anything for love, but deep down he's more comfortable alone. So he picks relationships that simply don't work, or he picks someone unavailable or whom he doesn't love. There always seems to be an excuse or a detour that prevents the conscious goal from materializing, but it's merely the deeper unconscious program that's manifesting, much like a law.

As we are—coming from the ego—it's hard to create cleanly. The deeper programs and drives will continue to eclipse the rather feeble conscious mind.

Of course, these words will spark a tsunami of criticism. Thousands will say they that every one of these systems has helped them. I'm not saying all these methods are bad; everything has its place. If you believe you are your mind and body, then where else can you start? The mind does indeed have tremendous power over the body and emotions, but it's the unconscious mind that really matters, and superficial practices don't touch it.

There's also nothing wrong with a powerful, healthy ego, but building a powerful ego isn't awakening—it's ego development, which at best may make you rich, powerful, and super-functional in society. However, even if you achieve wealth, power, and recognition, it's likely you will still be on the treadmill, hoping to figure out how to find joy outside yourself. No matter how powerful the ego, it's still seeing life through a distorted lens.

That's why the methods outlined in this book have always been for the few. Most don't want to knock down the house; they just want to fix it up a little. Sometimes a person brings so much to the table that they have to talk about it, scream, hit a pillow, or cry just to relieve some pressure. And yes, those measures help people become more functional. If a person stops feeling depressed or stops wanting to punch one's boss in the face or kill oneself, that may help one to fit into society—but it's a sick society and only a remodel because it's still working with the ego. It's like installing a new window, putting down a rug, or adding a coat of paint; the house may be more livable, but it remains the same old place. With ego therapy, we may *think* we're liking ourselves better, but we're still working with the same ego, which isn't our real self to begin with. And under the pressure of intense fear or shock, it's easy to see that little has changed.

Ultimately the house of the ego is not fixable. If you explore it deeply enough, including the basement and sub-basement, you'll see there's no real way to dig out of the mess. At that point you don't try to change anything. You simply walk out of the dark, hopelessly cluttered room into the clear alive sunshine.

To repeat: any method is effective only to the degree that one goes inside, because only by deepening inner awareness can one truly transform. Methods of therapy performed by caring individuals may be beneficial simply because of the human element of care. A loving heart always helps! But to help beyond a functional level, a therapist should be skilled in steering the patient inside. Therapists should help the patient develop awareness of the real self, rather than merely console the ego.

When you come from the core, there's no need to keep renewing your intention or keep it in the forefront of your mind. The vision burns like a flame and broadcasts loud and clear from your center. The deepest desires of heart and soul make up the rudder that leads us through all the obscure bends and turns on the river of life. These deeper desires create and attract certain aspects of life to us much more than our minds do. The image we keep in the mind is only a reflection of the vision in the heart. And it is these deepest desires of heart and soul—rather than what many people mistakenly call "will"—that provide the enthusiasm to walk the path to the top of the mountain. But willpower is merely the dogged tenaciousness of the ego and is always inferior to the vision of the heart.

Going inside is not therapy. It's tearing down the false edifice that's been built. It's deprogramming the brainwashing you've received over a lifetime. It's developing awareness so that the scales fall from your eyes and you see what you really are. But to get through the valley of death and reach your core, you have to see everything that's holding you back. As B.K.S. Iyengar said, before we can understand our own soul, we must explore all that eclipses our true selves. It's not enough to control the mind and push away negative thoughts. Before you can transcend thoughts and feelings, they should be deeply explored.

Observation and Awareness

The only method is observation through the eyes of your inner self. *Okay, just watch and wait, sure,* you may be saying.

There must be more to it. What about the great secrets of enlightenment? That's exactly what the mind wants: a cookbook method that has a promise attached to it for you to focus on. The mind loves a recipe. If you do everything right, step by step, you will succeed. If you try harder and become a fanatic, the results will come even quicker.

Consider this story about a student who visits a meditation master. He asks all kinds of questions about what he must do to become enlightened. The master just nods his head and says, "The day is so hot—let me get you a drink of water." The master goes over to the stream and brings back a glass of water.

The student takes one look at the water with all the dirt and leaves floating in it and says: "I can't drink that. Didn't you see the horses and cart go by? They walked through the water and now the bottom is all stirred up."

The master wades into the stream and tries to pick out all the debris and brings him another glass of water.

The student shakes his head. "No, it's worse."

The master goes back and tries even harder to pick out all the particulate matter. He brings it back to the student, who shakes his head.

"You made it even worse," the student says. "Don't you see that all you have to do is wait and the water will clear by itself?"

"Oh, I see," the teacher says with a piercing gaze.

Does this lesson mean we should abandon effort? The

spiritual path is a paradox. Many meditation masters insist that all methods of awakening are useless and that effort is like pushing against a door that can only be pulled. In the purest sense, that's true. As soon as one desires truth, it becomes a goal to be achieved. To reach the goal, effort must be employed. Effort is surely required in the physical world. If you want to build your biceps, regular curls with weights will help. However, on the spiritual level, the same rules don't apply. Ultimately, goals and the effort to achieve them are impediments to truth. The harder you try, the more that truth eludes you. Desires, effort, and ideals keep you on a vicious hamster wheel of mental conflict, obscuring the real self to an even greater degree and keeping you separate from the whole. The final jump into the void, or the act of becoming one with life, requires only surrender, the opposite of effort.

But desire and effort are almost always the first leg of the journey. The desire to awaken, or to be fulfilled, is still a desire, and without effort, surrender will not be true. How does one go straight into surrender? The ego is boss, and the chance of its surrendering is like the chance for snow in July. We've been trained to believe that effort is what gets the prize. How can you say effort is no good until you've given something your full effort? Can you tell a beggar who has never had enough money that money won't bring happiness? Can you tell a teenage boy that sex with beautiful women won't make him happy? Of course not. One has to see that sex and money, though they may bring pleasure, are not the final answer to fulfillment. Words fall short; one must experience the limitations of these experiences for himself. Effort is necessary to getting to the final stage, where you can see the futility of effort. Effort creates the tension so you can finally let go into surrender.

Sincerity

The effort required on the spiritual path is sometimes called sincerity, or earnestness. There's an absolute truth: people do what they want. A friend of mine owns a general store in the country. Many people in the area receive government support and pay for their groceries with food stamps. My friend notes that though everyone claims to be broke, they always have cash for alcohol and cigarettes. People always have time and money for what they want the most.

You must want truth enough to keep awareness focused. Metaphorically, the state of desiring truth above all else is described as being on fire. If one is on fire, he will keep the essence of his being focused. Being lukewarm or half-assed won't be enough to light a flame, and we need the flame to burn brightly as we travel the path to the core.

Suggestions for Practice

Keep watching. Once it becomes a way of life, observation is almost a non-effort. And developing your inner awareness to greater and greater degrees could be called a non-method. As the flame of awareness burns more brightly, it penetrates the depths of the mind. Keep awareness honed and focused, and simply observe what's pulling you from clear consciousness.

Sri Nisargadatta Maharaj, in *I Am That*, said: "You must watch yourself continuously—particularly your mind—moment by moment, missing nothing. This witnessing is essential for the separation of the self from the not–self."

As consciousness gets more and more present, the pot gets stirred. You will see the ego mind for what it is. Change will occur naturally and without effort.

Sincerity Reality Check

Keep track of yourself during the day. How much of your consciousness is focused on the real self, and how much is focused on everyday affairs? Of course, we all have many chores and responsibilities to tend to, but those who seek in earnest will focus at least some attention on what the inner self is doing. On the other hand, those who are more interested in the outer world will be focused there. There's no right or wrong, better or worse; it's just where you are.

Chapter 9

Know Thyself: That Is . . . Know the Small Self

When you know the ego is messed up—and that no longer bothers you—you've taken a really big step.

To dethrone the ego mind, it has to be seen for what it is: a petty dictator that isn't worth taking seriously.

My daughter is five years old. When she doesn't get the toy she wants, she might get angry and tell me she hates me or I'm the worst father in the world. Every parent knows that such words are meaningless. Talk like that goes in one ear and out the other. After a few moments, she'll say, "I love you," and tell me I'm the greatest dad, which I don't take all that seriously either.

To de-power the mind as master and make it no more than a willful child entails taking a good look. Not an intellectual look but rather an increasing inner awareness in which the presence of clear consciousness becomes stronger. You (consciousness) go progressively deeper inside. You walk through the valley of death and observe all the many layers of conditioning and programming that have been fed to you. On the road to the core, you'll experience your wounds, insecurities, desires, and fears. As you observe with the inner eyes, the charge is taken from your thoughts and you stop identifying with them. This process takes much awareness because the E.F. Hutton phenomenon runs so deep, but each time your inner self clearly witnesses the ego mind, you believe in its voice less and less. As thought waves become less powerful, they naturally decrease in strength and amplitude and become less jarring to the nervous system.

The mind, however, is tricky business, and observation requires readiness, inner strength, and a gentle sense of humor. You have to give yourself permission to start cracking the nut. Serious people tend to get freaked out when they see their inner thoughts. If you want to imagine yourself as a good boy or girl—perfect, calm, sane, logical, collected, with your act together—cracking open the nut of your ego is going to shock the hell out of you.

The ego has been called the small self, and with observation, you'll clearly see why. The small self isn't so nice. You may secretly be happy about someone's misfortune or jealous of another's triumph. Maybe you wish the old aunt would finally croak so you can collect the inheritance, or the beautiful girl would get fat or break out in acne so you can be more beautiful than she is. And that's just the tip of the iceberg; deeper programs will surface, such as prejudice. You might be talking to your neighbor, a Jewish person, and think: *Cheap Jew! They have all the damn money.* Your heart jumps. Where did that come from? Truth is, you like old neighbor Feinstein, and, consciously, you aren't against anyone. Words like that are foreign to you. It's as if a voice has been planted in your head. And it *has* been planted—through decades, even generations, of insidious brainwashing. And there will be many more voices, such as the no-saying voice of fear and insecurities that limit our lives.

The No-saying Voice

We try to tell ourselves we're wonderful, everyone loves us, and we can do anything. But then there's the small but persistent voice of the ego that is secretly insecure. This is the voice that says no to life. It's important to see just how many times your ego whispers that you can't, that you're not good enough, that you need to quit—and then to note the feelings of sadness, apathy, or depression that follow.

That's one reason I've always loved the martial arts. The nature of constant competition draws out the no-saying voice that one usually isn't even aware of. "'He's better than me; I'll never win," plays in the background. Even the best fighters in the world have confessed that the night before a fight they wonder if they'll be good enough. As a fighter, when you're exhausted and out of breath, there's the voice that whispers that you have to quit. The beauty of the martial arts is that you'll hear the no-saying voice enough times to realize it's just a puff of air. It's there, but you don't have to identify with it. Slap hands and get down to it.

Most never actualize their potential in life, simply because the no-saying voice intimidates them. They even put stops on good ideas before they actualize. It's a fact that those who succeed in life "just do it." They take action and complete their projects regardless of the no-saying voice.

The Subconscious Sexual Voice

Psychology tells us that we have sexual thoughts hundreds if not thousands of times a day. Indeed, the more the witness is present, the more you will see how much sexual thoughts, fantasies, and sexual prejudices rule the mind. Sex is perhaps the most powerful drive on earth and can easily pull you from awareness. Sexual attraction is all-consuming, but who is attracted? At the core, of course, is biology. Then, layered on top of nature's instinct to propagate the species, are the ego's particular sexual preferences and expressions. It's common to appraise each eligible person as a potential sexual or marriage partner. Just listen to your inner dialogue around sex as you see someone who holds attraction for you or one who repulses you.

The Ego Thrives on Conflict

The ego enjoys creating shocking thoughts, because throwing a wrench into the works only increases conflict, therefore amplifying the ego's power. Ego thrives on conflict, much like a top has to spin to remain upright. If movement stops, the top will fall. The ego doesn't want to fall. It has a survival consciousness and will fight you desperately. With the many years you've spent building the house of the ego, you think it *is* you. Any blow to the ego's survival is an assault on the survival of *you*, and so the ego upholds itself—the false you—with every trick it possesses.

Let's say you're sitting in church and everything's nice, but then you have the thought you'd like to have sex with the preacher right on the pulpit. Or you're holding your aunt's baby and your mind says, *What if I drop it*? Or maybe you're feeling depressed and the mind whispers that it would be best if you took your own life. Then the mind will spin webs and create scenarios. "If I drop the baby, everyone will be mad and think I'm a bad person." "If I kill myself, my boyfriend will be sad . . . or maybe he'll be with Mary Ellen by next week!" Or "What will everyone say about me at my funeral?"

With a bit of observation, you'll see that some thoughts are not at all pretty, but we can't pretend that they don't exist in the collective ego mind. After working with thousands of people, I know the mind's voices can sometimes be so clear, shocking, and outrageous that they can frighten the heck out of you. Some attribute those voices to the devil, a discarnate entity, or a psychological disorder for which medication is needed. More often than not, however, the voice inside originates from the crowd of unexplored or implanted voices in your own mind. Never forget: the ego thrives on conflict. The mind has been in charge for so long it wants to stay that way and will fight tooth and nail to do so.

The Sea Gives Up Her Dead Only When Ready

If any of your desires, ugliness, smallness, aggressions to hurt or even kill others, deep depression, despair, or thoughts of suicide shock you or you think you're evil or a bad person and you frantically pray or push disturbing thoughts away as "improper," you're giving a signal that you're not ready to see. In the future, you're likely to censor or shunt such thoughts.

There's an old saying among sailor folk: "The sea only gives up her dead when she's ready." Sailors noted that when a man drowned, his body might immediately float up to the surface, or in some cases a bloated old body would float to the surface after being underwater for many days. Still others might rest at the bottom of the sea, never coming up again. Why the sea holds her dead is a mystery. But anyone who sails knows the sea has a soul, and so it is assumed she holds her dead until she is ready to let them go. The same fascinating phenomenon happens in your body with toxins, and in your mind with fear.

A major tenet of natural medicine is that the body tries to maintain balance by eliminating whatever is harmful to it—but there's a limit. If toxins are taken in beyond the body's capacity to remove them, they are walled off and stored, usually in the most susceptible tissues and organs. When the system gains sufficient vitality, through regimens of cleansing and building that use nutrition, exercise, and detoxification, the body develops the strength to expel these old toxins. A century ago, the mysterious expulsion of old, walled-off toxic material was called a healing crisis, and a Norwegian homeopath named Herring observed a definite order to this phenomenon: disease is cured from the head down, from the inside out, and from the reverse order in which it came. Using Herring's law of cure, we find that the oldest and most deeply seated poisons are the last to be expelled. However, it may take years to build up the necessary vitality to do so.

The mind is perhaps even more sophisticated than the body in its repression of toxic material. It's a common story: a woman was raped when she was young, never told anyone, and seemingly forgot all abut it. Then, years later, when in a more emotionally secure place, she is triggered by seeing, hearing, or smelling something that brings her back to the original incident. After remembering some of the repressed material, she pieces the rest together, or the memories may all come back at once.

Some believe that the concept of repressed memories is no more than a bogus theory hatched by Freud. Critics point to the fact that people remember things that never happened, due to misperception and misinterpretation of the actual events. Planting suggestions in someone's mind is also quite real. In recent years, cases of repressed sexual abuse have become so frequent that therapists have been cautioned not to inadvertently suggest that one may have been sexually abused.

While it's true that the perception and interpretation of past events are always suspect and that suggestion can certainly influence the mind, my experience with patients has shown that there are many defense mechanisms in our bodies and minds. What can't be handled will somehow be repressed. It seems to be a law of nature and is a very deep survival mechanism.

Until you are ready to navigate the depths, you will be able to observe only the most superficial layers of your mind. If the more sensitive, ugly, or disconcerting aspects surface, they'll retreat right back into the dark basement of your unconscious. It may seem a terrible amount of unnecessary work to introvert yourself through the observation process, but only when we allow the unconscious to rise to the surface do we realize the possibility to be free from ourselves.

Cracking the Nut Begins with Acceptance and Humor

These are the Three Acceptances: *accept yourself, accept everything you have done, and accept what life has given you.*

The most basic honesty is to be yourself. There's no use in pretending to be what you aren't, trying to live up to what you ought to be, or repressing what you are. That only causes inner conflict. To dive deep, begin with acceptance. There's a tremendous power in simply being *you*. It's the only possible starting point, because it takes the path of least resistance. If you can't accept yourself, it's a mental fight.

Acceptance might be called the 101 of growth because unification is the first step. In his book *Kundalini Tantra*, Swami Satyananda Saraswati discusses the psychology of total acceptance in relationship to the mind:

> Suppressing the mind and calling it back again and again is not the way to concentrate the mind, it is a way to the mental hospital. After all, who suppresses or calls back who? Are there two personalities or two minds in you? Is there one bad mind that keeps wandering off and one good mind which tries to bring

back the bad mind? No, there is only one mind and you should not create a split by antagonizing the mind. If you do this one part of the mind becomes dictator and controller and the other part becomes the victim. Then you'll develop a great gap between two aspects of your mind and personality and within a very short time become totally schizophrenic.

On some meditative paths, you might get the impression that the goal is to kill the ego. But even the ego isn't something to be despised; it's not an enemy, and hating any part of yourself is counterproductive. The idea isn't to destroy or cut out any part of you. If you do, you're no longer whole, and fighting—with any part of you—keeps you conflicted. Again, be gentle with yourself. Do nothing with the mind—just let the ego be as it is. In a way, the ego has been our friend. The ego egg has insulated us; it's protected us from getting into waters too deep to swim. But as the presence of consciousness gets stronger, you may be ready to handle greater depths.

The Big Show

Nonacceptance can be subtle. By trying to be something you're not, by putting on a false face—something most of us do for much of our lives—you're not accepting who you are.

Expectations, standards of excellence, compel us to live

up to the ideal—even if it's a farce. We learn this behavior in early childhood, when we're rewarded for being good girls or helpful, happy boys. We like the positive reinforcement and the warmth we receive, so we learn to be actors. We learn to be false. Most people wear so many faces that the real person is invisible. Just like people start to believe their fish stories, they come to believe they are their masks. Decades later, adults still try to uphold the image of the happy, helpful boy or the good girl—and they still like to be praised for it.

The mask is simply the disparity between the image you're presenting to the world—what you want everyone to see—and what you secretly feel. The show you put on is the opposite of how the small self really feels. If it feels weak, it pretends to be strong; the most macho show of confidence is usually covering insecurity. If not good enough, it wants everyone to think it's brilliant and special; if it feels ugly, it wants to be seen as beautiful; if it feels unloved, it wants to be cherished; if insignificant, it wants to be the most important thing on the planet.

With clear observation, you'll see how you do and say things to uphold the persona of your mask. And, of course, you wear different masks depending on who's standing in front of you. You'll put on different faces for your boss—someone you're trying to impress—and a beggar on the street. You'll show one face to someone who's attractive to you and a different one to someone who turns you off. Watch carefully: many times we aren't even aware how much tension and energy wearing our masks takes. Keeping up our facade is tiresome, and, of course, there's the fear that the truth will be discovered.

The Big Show is in full force when you meet someone you like. You want him or her to think you are Mr. or Ms. Right, but sooner or later, the truth of who you are will be discovered. Self-help and relationship guru Bob Mandel used to suggest putting your worst foot forward on the first date; in other words, skip the drama and start by being your genuine self. Take off the masks and be exactly who you are without apologies. It'll be better in the long run. If you don't know who you really are, use inner awareness to see whether the face you're presenting is real. Oftentimes one is the most real when completely alone. When no one's watching, there's no need for masks.

The Perfect Trap

Trying to attain perfection is a sure way to *not* be who you are. It only creates guilt, tension, and chaos. Examining your outer behavior to become a better person is also a setup for failure. So is scrutinizing each day and judging if you did well or badly. You'll never be at peace with these methods; you'll be like a dog chasing its tail. When you slip, you're just going to rip yourself apart, vow never to do it again, and lose confidence when you do. This crazy cycle is precisely what's going to keep the ego fat and sassy.

Take Responsibility

Another shade of acceptance is to take responsibility for your life. It can be hard to accept, but no one in the world is a real victim of life. Some may appear to be—they may have been wronged, or perpetrated against by a person, organization, or country—but they still are not victims of life. We may not be to blame, but still we must accept what life has given us. There's a deeper principle at work. Our own field of energy creates our life. How can it be otherwise? If you put a cutout of a bat over a flashlight and shine the light on the wall, it's no surprise to see the image of a bat on the wall. As the energy of life shines through our own energy field, we create the conditions to match our consciousness.

As the presence of your consciousness becomes stronger, it penetrates deeper and deeper through the distortions in your mind. The method is simple—*awareness*—but there's a caution: don't get into this process with a male mind or super-serious attitude. It's easy to get fanatical with any method, but it's better to be relaxed and easy with yourself. Approach the process as feminine: watch everything that goes on in your mind with gentle amusement—without judgment. If you get sucked into the drama and lose awareness, call the witness back to the body and watch again.

Suggestions for Practice

Integrate the three acceptances; accept yourself as you are, everything you've ever done, and what life provides. Simply be who you are without apologies. Take responsibility for your life.

Continue to observe the ego mind with compassionate awareness. Remember that when the witness is present and you are able to observe the mind, you are most likely in the body. When caught in strong thoughts, you are probably out of your body. Continue to bring clear consciousness back again and again. Keeping consciousness in the forefront at all times is the best meditation. From the instant your eyes open in the morning, watch the habitual programming of your mind. What are the first words that spring from your mind as you rise out of bed and begin your day? Do these thoughts serve you and do you want to program yourself with them? Don't be shocked or try to positive-think or neutralize your thoughts in any way. Just watch, gently.

Don't fight with the mind, just let it be. As you watch the mind without judgment, you'll see that it rehashes the same boring story over and over. The more your real self watches it, the less you identify with anything that goes on in your mind. As awareness deepens, you should begin to question the veracity of your thoughts. If they're coming from the ego mind, just how reliable is the source? No matter how ugly, never shy away from what's going on inside you. Whatever comes up, accept it without judgment. Adopt the attitude of a plumber rooting in a clogged toilet: he's seen so much crap in his life that it doesn't bother him anymore. Even if he gets shit on his skin, he's nonplussed, still pleasant and jovial. Try to have fun with this journey; separating the real from the false is a fascinating endeavor. Playing and watching with amusement gives your unconscious the signal that you're ready to see. An inner gate opens and the dregs of the mind start rising like bubbles from the muddy bottom of a lake.

As you watch these bubbles, you'll see they are no more than old, dead echoes. Your mind isn't you; thoughts are not you, nor are they even yours. Thoughts come from the mental field of energy and are everyone's property. Thoughts arise like the noise that spews from a talking toy when you hit the button. The mind is movement. It will never stop making waves, even after awakening. Thoughts come and go, but the reaction to them lessens.

Chapter 10

Going Deeper with the Fast Path

It may take time to develop the presence of the inner self to the degree that you penetrate your ego and see it for what it is. It also takes a great deal of courage and fortitude. If you've stuck with this up till now, you'll experience times when observing the mind comes easily. Usually, the superficial thoughts that have the least charge can be watched with detached amusement. You may be able to laugh at the games and shenanigans of the mind, and that's good progress.

Observing the mind through the eyes of the witness without pushing stuff under the rug is an important step. Even if you get only to the point where you see the foibles of the mind, you've done well. You'll probably take yourself a lot less seriously. Most people, however, stop there. It's a safe spot.

You haven't gone into the place of no return, where you see the real chaos of the mind. Once you do, you'll never be quite comfortable in your old world again. For those who want to go further, the fast path lights a fire underneath you that helps bring you to the boiling point.

Calling it the fast path, however, is a misnomer. There are no real shortcuts. No one knows how long it will take to penetrate the ego mind so that you're ready to surrender. It could be now, many years from now, or many lifetimes. The fast path is merely a concentrated look inside.

Older cultures had practical, intensive ways of dealing with the ego. Tibetan lamas were known to put a student in a dark room for many months. In some cases they stayed isolated in darkness for an entire lifetime. Each day the candidates would receive a small amount of food pushed through the door. Native Americans use vision quests. After the appropriate purifications, such as a sweat-lodge ceremony, one is isolated on a confined spot on the land. For one to forty days, no food is taken, and for lesser durations, no water. The Peruvian shamans guide one through a *dieta*, where one is alone in a *tambo*, an open-air hut in the jungle. One eats only small amounts of rice and green plantains and perhaps a little fish. One is given powerful herbs to help facilitate the going-inside process.

The various disciplines each have a unique flavor that takes one into a non-ordinary state of consciousness. The Tibetan method uses complete isolation in darkness. There's no company, not even a plant. The Native American method uses fasting. When food is completely withheld, the body weakens and one turns more intensely inward to thought and emotion. If you fast, you will see—if you don't know already—to what degree thoughts of food are part of your consciousness. In contrast with the Tibetan method, the vision quest puts one outside in direct contact with nature. The Amazon approach also uses the outdoors, and the herbs consumed force one to turn inward. The similarities, however, are more important than the differences.

The common thread in such an experience is that you're taken away from your life, which helps you to go inside. No distractions are allowed. Books, music, computers, cell phones—all are taboo. Even talking isn't allowed much, if at all. There's nothing to do. Perhaps for the first time in your life, you're giving yourself the opportunity to do nothing. One would imagine it would be a good time to relax, but relaxation usually doesn't happen. At first, perhaps, you might be bored. Maybe you sleep a lot for a couple of days, but you can't sleep forever, especially if you're not eating or the food is sparse. Food can act like a drug, and lack of it facilitates less and lighter sleep.

Eventually, you must cozy up to the rambling in your head. If you are ready, all the ghosts you have pushed away into the basement of your mind will come to haunt you. A whole lifetime of ghosts may come knocking. It's so quiet where you are, but their voices seem awfully loud and jarring. Very soon, you wish you could turn the voices off, but you can't. You'll see that the voices in your head aren't your own but rather a crowd of voices that have come from others. Voices from your family, society, clergy—expectations, guilt, and shame trips—as well as from television advertising slogans. You'll see that you're a collection, a montage of brainwashing fueled by other people's projections, all held together with your formative trauma.

The voices go on and on, and with nothing else to do, you're forced to see all the foibles of your identity, all the neuroses that make up your personality. The unconscious drives, superstitions, sexual desires, and fantasies as well as the games and chaos you are compelled to create to validate your small self and make your unconscious patterns a reality.

Step onto the fast path and you'll wonder how you've pushed away all this chaos for so long. Somehow you've managed to avoid it, to divert it through school, work, friends, books, music, sex, exercise, the Internet, television, gambling, alcohol, drugs, the pursuit of spirituality, or a hundred other distractions. But now there is nothing to distract. You believed your mind was logical, rational, and clear, but now you see it to be fragmented—an erratic, free-associating nightmare. One stray thought starts a chain of thoughts that the mind weaves into entire stories. These stories may seem like nonsense, but they reveal how your mind works and how your ego has been formed. You'll want to move, to work, to find something, but there's nothing to do.

Suggestions for Practice

One Day

Give yourself one day with nothing but a pad of paper and a pen. It will seem tedious, but write down every single thought you have for at least three hours. If you can manage a full day, even better. This simple exercise will reveal many of your inner patterns and how tedious and boring the ruts of your mind are. It will also convince you of the flightiness of the mind. Read over what you've written. Be honest. Do you want the mind to sit in the general's chair and call the shots?

Be with Yourself

Take one day to a full week and pick a spot in nature. Fast or eat very lightly and just sit with yourself, watching the mind. Leave behind distractions such as books, music, and your phone or other electronics. It's okay to write in a journal, do artwork, or occasionally play a musical instrument, because these activities can be cathartic by helping hidden data in the unconscious mind to rise to the surface, where it can be seen.

Don't get discouraged. Many report that their first vision quest does nothing but reveal their inner stuckness and misery. But seeing this is a wonderful and necessary step.

Ask Yourself a Question

The mind is amazing. One stray thought can turn into an entire "what if" story.

Say you're sitting in a park at dusk; not too many people are there. You see a homeless man pushing a cart filled with bottles. He's young and wouldn't be that bad-looking if he'd clean up a little. All of a sudden, you wonder if you should really be sitting here all alone. What if he's a bad man? And speaking of bad, tomorrow is going to suck. Why in the world did you stack so many appointments so close together? What if you make a mistake and someone sees you're not as good as everyone thinks you are? And last weekend at the party, when Jessica said it looked like you'd gained a few pounds, you should've come up with a wittier comeback than "Isn't that the pot calling the kettle black?" Especially since that African-American girl, Sara, was standing right there. She probably thinks you're a racist. Stupid! You made yourself look like a fool. Next time Jessica calls, you have to remember that that fat two-faced bitch isn't your friend. She doesn't like you, so you're not going to like her either.

When you are sucked into a long trail of thoughts that turn into a "what if" story, ask yourself: Where were you during this time? Where did your clear consciousness go?

Explore Fear

Sooner or later, fear comes. When your facade of logic bursts, you will tap into your fear. If you're not protecting yourself, it can't be avoided. You will clearly see just how illogical, and irrational your mind is; you may think that if you have one more thought you may actually lose your mind. The safety of your ego is threatened. You are now on the brink of entering the deeper elements of your mind. The elemental fear you experience at this junction might even be called the glue of your ego.

Now is when you pay even more attention to keeping yourself in the body and opening the eyes of awareness.

PART 5

Unraveling the Glue of the Ego

Chapter 11

Unconscious Shock

THERE ARE THOUSANDS OF SPIRITUAL BOOKS ADVISING US to stay in the now, live in peace, and open our hearts. Have you ever wondered why it's difficult to actually do so? An open, loving heart is our natural state, but you can't force or will your heart to open. The heart opens spontaneously when you loosen the factors blocking it. Awakening also happens naturally when you see that the obstacles to awareness aren't real, which means going all the way through the valley of death to your core. Sooner or later on this road, you're going to run smack into unconscious shock.

Back in Chapter 5, I mentioned that leaving the body is the most misunderstood phenomena in health care and spirituality. Shock is the other half of that equation:

unconscious shock is the trigger that causes us to leave the body in the first place.

Maybe at this point you can observe your everyday mind without losing your real self. Perhaps you can retain awareness even when someone criticizes you, steps on your tail, or cuts you off on the highway. That's fantastic progress, but as the practice of observation takes you deeper and deeper into the mind, you'll experience times when what's going on in your mind is so compelling—or evokes such discomfort—that you're sucked into it. Inner receptivity takes the exit ramp and consciousness vanishes. The most difficult time for anyone to maintain conscious awareness is during times of deep elemental fear.

Though we all have it, fear is often misunderstood. Fear may not arise from something tangible, such as a snake about to bite, but as a reaction to something that happened a long time ago. I once studied with William Emerson, a pre- and perinatal psychologist who pioneered the shock model of psychotherapy. Emerson observed that some emotionally triggered patients exhibited the exact signs and symptoms of a severe stress reaction. They might have experienced reduced skin temperature, changes in heart rate, blood pressure, or respiration, and other symptoms of acute sympathetic nervous system arousal (such as freezing and going into a confused or paralyzed mental state—unable to take action or even move). Yet there was no danger. Nothing external had happened to cause it. The apparent shock came in reaction to something occurring internally. Emerson realized that the individual had been triggered and reactivated into shock by something that had happened in the past.

***NB: *My understanding of shock may not be what Dr. Emerson or anyone else believes about mental/emotional shock.*

Shock and Leaving the Body: The Missing Diagnosis

Psychology understands that a traumatic incident may cause a person's mind to split, depersonalize, disassociate, isolate, become aggressive, obsess, or any of the various psychological labels, but it doesn't take into consideration the shaman's or the meditator's point of view that spirit, the true being, is simply not at home in the body.

To get the complete picture, one must understand that mental/emotional shock disposes the real self, or consciousness, to vacate the body. It's perfectly natural. When faced with severe trauma, the inner self takes flight to protect one from experiencing the brunt of the incident. Shock, however, stays in the system and triggers us to habitually leave the body, causing what the shamans call soul loss. Ultimately, all the psychological diagnoses are caused by various degrees of soul loss (being out of the body and entangled with another person, a place in time, or even a dimension).

The shaman's definition may seem unscientific, esoteric, and downright ridiculous, but think about it. Unresolved shock and trauma cause one to continually revisit the incident in an attempt to resolve it. For example, say a girl suffered abuse by her dad in her childhood home, in Toledo, Ohio, in 1966. If that wound remains unhealed, she remains enmeshed with her father. Part of her stays stuck in 1966, back at that home in Ohio. Even if the home is no longer there and her dad has died, part of her stays tied up in it. And there's that much less of her present now to experience life. However, to say that the spirit is entangled is not quite accurate. It may seem as if one's spirit is tangled with another, but spirit is free. It's the ego mind, the person, that becomes tangled, which results in a loss of presence or clear consciousness.

The Formation of a Shock Wound

Physical injuries are well-understood. A force hitting our bodies—a baseball, a fist, or stairs as we fall down them—will cause swelling, bruises, lacerations, torn ligaments, and broken bones. But what is wounded in a non-physical injury such as shock or trauma?

First of all, shock is more severe when it's unexpected. Those who don't experience an incident as overwhelming—usually because they anticipated it or consciously perceive it while it's happening—don't flee from their bodies. They have far less reaction because when the outer and inner selves are aligned, it is naturally protective. The one person who manages to stay in his body during a bad car crash can help the others because he isn't frozen in shock. Nor does that person retain the same degree of psychic damage.

John Upledger, a DO in Somato Emotional Release, notes that if one gets injured slipping on a patch of ice while laughing it up with a friend (laughing usually grounds us in the body), the injury will leave much less physical/mental/emotional damage than if one has the exact same injury while in a fearful or angry state of mind (out of the body). Upledger observed that a shocking or traumatic incident may leave a residue in the body, which he calls an energy cyst. The cyst may lodge itself in any organ or tissue and broadcast its own energy, which disrupts the overall flow of energy in the body. German New Medicine believes that shock creates an impression on the brain in the form of concentric circles. The imprint will predictably affect a certain organ, depending on the embryonic part of the brain involved.

The phenomenon of how shock imprints the brain and affects the physical body is cutting-edge medicine and may be explained in different ways. I like to think about it energetically. When out of the body, one is more or less a ship without a captain, and more susceptible to mental/emotional injury. Fear, although unseen with the physical eyes, is an extremely powerful energy that cuts deeply. As shock ensues, the mind literally folds in on itself. A mental/emotional knot is formed. Trapped within the knot are emotions, memories, colors, smells, sounds, and images—whatever happened at the time of injury. In other words, emotions can be stuck in the energetic field, attached to physical tissue, or tied to an organ such as the heart or kidneys. The shock complex interferes with the circulation and free flow of energy because it immediately activates the sympathetic nervous system. The physical body, under powerful, prolonged sympathetic stimulation, will almost always develop chronic health problems.

A major shock forms a wrinkle or groove in the mind that can be easily activated and entered into. The deeper the groove, the more one is pulled into it. While mentally revisiting the incident, one is occupied. Clear consciousness is gone. The more entangled a person is in past events, the less she is at home in the body and the less she is capable of living in the now. Occulted (hidden, repressed, or unknown) shock may cripple our lives even more than that which is known. Known or not, shock activates the nervous system, resulting not only in tension and anxiety but also a crimping of inner circulation. Occulted shock remains a trigger that causes us to leave the body.

What psychology labels "abnormal" behavior could be considered quite normal, in the sense that such behaviors are adopted in an attempt to protect oneself and find a safe place to survive. Disassociation and depersonalization, split personality, bipolar disorder, obsessive-compulsive disorder, and borderline personality disorders can all be explained in relation to the psyche's reaction to shock. The mind may dissociate, split, obsess, and so on, but these are all self-protective attempts at dealing with shock.

Shock may be so great that it overshadows one's entire life. In cases of severe shock, a shaman might say that the spirit has gone so far away that it may never come back. I suggest that shock can create such a massive wrinkle or knot in the mind that one gets stuck there and can't get out. Consciousness is so severely estranged that it becomes inaccessible. The words are slightly different, but they amount to the same thing: the real self isn't at home.

What Exactly Is Shock?

Shock might be thought of as the offspring of intense fear. It's a reaction to the highest level of perceived danger. In grading shock as compared with trauma, the most severe levels of trauma just begin to approach the lowest level of shock.

What stimulates terror so great that it becomes shock? That depends. Being held up at gunpoint would clearly be shocking, but there are many less obvious threats to physical, emotional, or mental survival. When the great stock market crash occurred in 1929, some people in New York City were so shaken that they committed suicide by jumping out of their office windows. Divorce or death of one's partner can elicit shock in some, while losing face might be shocking to others. A surprise medical diagnosis such as terminal cancer may also be threatening enough to cause shock. Again, perception is everything. What may register as shock for one person might be innocuous for another. An important criterion, however, is powerlessness: the more helpless you feel and the fewer resources you have to defend yourself, the more shocking a particular stressor might be. (Perception of powerlessness is directly proportional to how grounded we are in our bodies.)

A newborn baby left unattended in a cold room for several hours might become so frightened that she could die. Even if there's no apparent harm, it will probably be a major shock to the psyche. A newborn is powerless; she can't do anything for herself, not even turn over. The discomfort of the cold room, the longing for security and the comfort of her mother, combined with the complete inability to help herself, can elicit shock. But leave a two-year-old for a few hours and the shock will probably be far less. A two-year-old can walk around and cry for help. If cold, he may have the presence of mind to get under the covers and go to sleep. Lock a teenager or an adult in a cold room, and it will probably be mildly stressful. Both would find ways to cope. Some might even enjoy it. And, of course, if they really wanted to get out, they could use the window or break down the door. The perception of danger is an important yardstick in determining how severe the shock is. And perception of danger greatly corresponds with our resources for handling it.

When completely overwhelmed at any age, one may go into shock. But shock wounds frequently occur in the womb or during birth, precisely because the fetus has such few resources. What can a fetus do when faced with perceived danger? Leaving the body, the outward flight of consciousness, is the only defense it has. In cases of toxic wombs, where the mom is anxious or circumstances cause repetitive stress or worry to the mom, leaving the body becomes hardwired as a survival mechanism.

Fetuses under chronic stress in the womb learn to energetically flee and, after birth, are more sensitive to noise and being startled. When under stress, the heart beats more quickly and forcefully than in an infant who spent a more relaxing time in the womb. Cardiac sensitivity, an exaggerated startle reflex, and other sensitivities persist throughout life, showing the link between early shock and the ramifications for the sympathetic nervous system.

The pre- and perinatal shock model explains why some are much more easily activated into a stress response than others, why an athlete who is extremely proficient in the gym might choke in competition, or why anyone may become overwhelmed and freeze in any of life's situations. Shock sheds light on why some feel nervous and uncomfortable inside when there's no apparent reason. Perhaps nothing terrible happened in someone's childhood, and yet he never feels quite right in his skin. Many people's lives are a direct reflection of their early shock. The same patterns play out again and again. However, pre- and perinatal shock wounds can be subtle and so far removed that neither patient nor therapist understands where they came from.

For example, people who had difficult births may experience a mysterious reluctance each time they begin a journey or a project. They may have a strange feeling of aversion or dread, as if taking the next step forward will be difficult or unpleasant. If a mother is in great distress during pregnancy because her husband is missing at war, perhaps that fear will be transferred to the baby. As the child grows, she may have an inordinate dread if Mom or Dad comes home late or if she has to stay home alone. Additionally, most pre- and perinatal psychologists believe that if a pregnant mom has even a passing thought of abortion, it can shock the fetus, which is why the job of an aware man is to help facilitate a garden of peace and joy for the pregnant mother. Though we're all responsible for our own states of consciousness, if a man can support the mother's harmony, her consciousness can turn, unfettered, to the new life within her body.

Conception wounds can be even vaguer. At the time of conception, a Chinese couple wish for a boy. Nine months later, a girl comes. Mother and father love and care for their daughter. She doesn't know they were disappointed by her gender, and yet she has a deep inexplicable feeling of being wrong. The conception shock of being wrong follows her around like a shadow. It plays out that she's the wrong person for the job, the wrong partner, and so on.

Pre- and perinatal shock isn't always a good fit for conventional therapies. Few professionals have been trained in the shock model—or shamanism—so no one quite understands where the problem is coming from. Patients don't remember the shock from the pre- and perinatal stages; they just know certain situations make them feel very uncomfortable inside—and so everyone is clueless.

I was one of those shocked souls. I had great parents and a wonderful childhood, but inside I was anxious and no one knew what was wrong. Take a look at this picture of me taken just a short while after I was born. You can see the marks on my temples from the long forceps. Look at my left arm, almost black from getting stuck in my mom's pelvis. Getting caught like this was one of the reasons I was such a shocked baby and why I had three near-death experiences. (One repeatedly re-creates trauma and shock so it can heal.) Last, cover my entire face except for the eyes. Does that look like the face of an infant who spent a happy, peaceful time in the womb? No, it's an infant frightened so severely that the eyes look like they come from two different people. One side looks angry, whereas the other side looks abjectly fearful. As I grew, I found ways to cope, but the latent shock

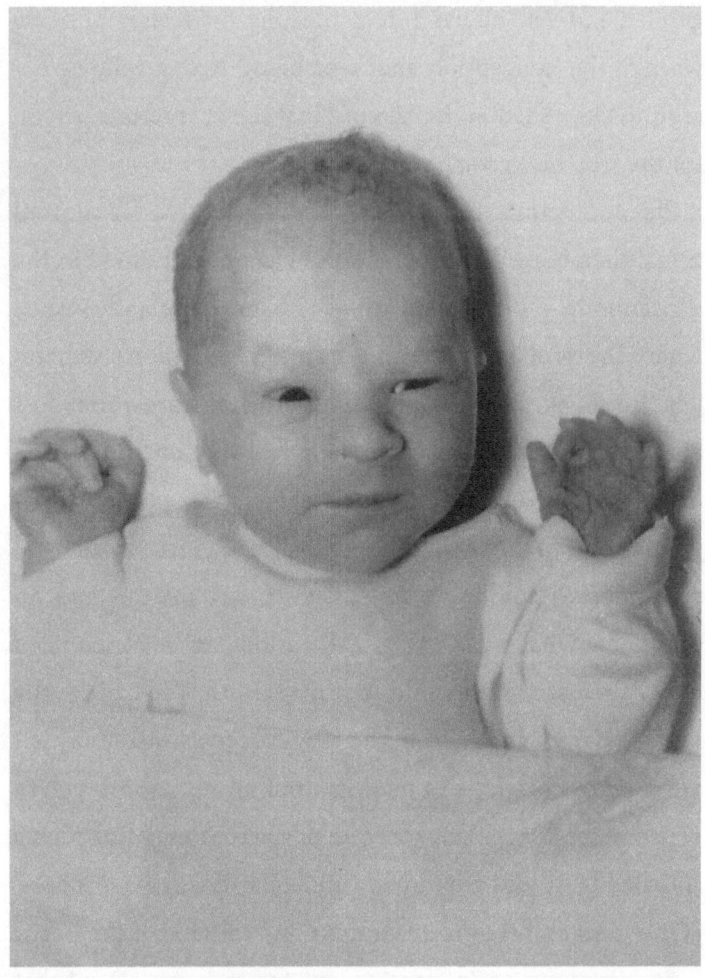

remained in my energetic field and nervous system, as it does with everyone.

I had a high IQ but performed miserably in school; I was hyperactive and had difficulty focusing. I was labeled a chronic underachiever. On the advice of physicians and psychologists, I was given drugs to calm me down, probably the predecessors of Ritalin. Of course, they didn't work.

Early shock seems to contribute to the degree of shock one experiences from trauma suffered later in life. It seems a mystery why some experience fear for no apparent reason, or when they never did before. You sometimes see this in the fight game. A previously undefeated, seemingly fearless fighter suffers a brutal beating in the ring. He tries to fight again, but everyone can see he's a different man. Something inside him has left. It's more than the beating he received, more than loss of confidence. The new shock complex taps into the old shock pool and touches on his elemental, primal shock. They are now inseparable.

Shock: The Portal to Growth

Everyone has a certain level of shock, but in the deepest sense, it's not at all negative. Life always gives us exactly what we need to grow. Pleasant times may be enjoyable, but shock, like a cattle prod, forces us to move beyond our comfort zones. Our particular shock becomes our unique template for growth. It is the friction point, the portal we must pass through to awaken and live fully.

Suggestions for Practice

A common self-help technique is to ask what your life would look like if there were no restrictions. If there were nothing to hold you back, where would you be? It's easy to conjure up multiple excuses for why we can't fulfill our dreams, such as physical attributes, unlucky breaks, or age. But look more closely. It's almost always fear that prevents us from living as fully as possible. Assuming that fear is preventing you from going all the way in any aspect of life—be it love, career, or the spiritual path—ponder where shock might be holding you back. If you haven't found your right partner or haven't been able to reach your dreams, whatever they may be, look to exploring shock around those areas.

Amp Up Awareness

Many push away fear for their entire lives and never get to the core of themselves, where they can see that fear isn't real. Start by bringing conscious awareness into times of fear and times when you're activated into shock. What's going on? Of course, you will be out of the body, but gently try to bring yourself back.

Singing Rocking Chair

This is a variation on a Native American ritual, a gentle method of beginning to go inside of pain and shock. When activated by pain, sit in a rocking chair and begin rocking back and forth. Remove external distractions. Give yourself permission to enter into the emotion as deeply as possible. Let whatever pain, fear, and uneasiness you feel wash over you. Put the pain or feeling into a song. You don't have to think much about it—just let the words pour out. Even if it's more like a chant, or one word over and over, like *stupid, fool, why me,* or *pain, pain, pain,* just surrender and let whatever wants to be expressed come out. Surrender yourself deeper and deeper into the feeling. Stop whenever it feels right, and sit and rock for a few minutes. Afterward, put down a blanket, lie on the ground, and surrender into the earth; sit up with your back against a tree; or take a walk in nature to integrate your feelings.

Give Yourself a Break

We've all made mistakes and lost opportunities because of fear. It's easy to beat ourselves up. If you look carefully at anyone's life, you'll see that many of the things they've done were protective mechanisms to avoid feeling shock. In many cases, those mechanisms were necessary to survival. Give yourself a break: accept where you are and what you've done in the past, and move on from there. As the presence of your awareness grows stronger, you'll be able to see shock for what it is and penetrate your coping mechanisms. But along the way, always be gentle and forgiving with yourself.

Chapter 12

Subtle Levels of Shock

Shock reaches from the misty beginnings of time, which is why fear is such a primal part of our psyche. This chapter explores the deeper levels of shock and explains why awakening is the only real cure for unconscious shock.

Ancestral Shock

Even if one doesn't believe in pre- and perinatal shock, the concept is easy enough to understand. The fetus directly experiences, reacts, and molds to the emotions of mother. What I call ancestral shock is even subtler and can affect you even though you seem to be completely removed from it. Trans-generational shock is one of the most mysterious types of shock because it doesn't happen directly to you. You probably don't even know how ancestral shock occurred or why it affects your life, but it may be responsible for deep inexplicable feelings, fears, and irrational drives and behaviors.

In the preface to *The Ancestor Syndrome*, by Anne Ancelin Schutzenberger, Nice Hyeres explains:

> The dead pass down to the living, according to Roman law. We continue the chain of generations and, knowingly or not, willingly or unwillingly, we pay debts of the past: as long as we have not cleared the slate, an "invisible loyalty" impels us to repeat and repeat a moment of incredible joy or unbearable sorrow, an injustice, or a tragic death. Or its echo.

Similarly, Hungarian psychoanalysts Abraham and Török introduced the concept of the "crypt" and the "phantom." The crypt is a dark secret that has been locked away and buried in the family system. The deed had to be ugly—or shocking—enough that it threatened the reputation, safety, security, or survival of an individual or the entire family. Acts of this nature are usually not spoken about and are eventually forgotten. Yet the shock that ripples through the family system doesn't end even after the family members who were responsible for the incident—or the victims of it—have died. Down the line, the secret mysteriously escapes from the crypt of the dead and inhabits the heart of the living. Descendants may repeat the fate of the dead ancestor, ancestors, or their victims, as if a ghost or phantom has possessed them, compelling them to move toward the same fate, even if such behavior is extremely uncharacteristic.

The crypt-and-phantom concept is similar to Bert Hellinger's concept of the family soul. If a tragedy, murder, or dark secret remains unresolved, then even after the death of those involved, a black hole forms in the family soul. (Perhaps Hellinger's black hole is the collective familial counterpart to German New Medicine's concentric circles that impress on the brain of an individual in response to personal shock.) The unresolved shock—be it an injustice, an unpaid debt, or a crime against humanity—acts like a curse and perpetuates itself through the generations. A deep elemental loyalty compels descendants born into the family to attempt to heal the disturbance. It seems that the most sensitive individuals take on and try to right the wrongs of past generations, but it's likely that ancestral shock is shared by everyone in the family, just in different ways and degrees.

The many manifestations and nuances of ancestral shock are difficult, if not impossible, to diagnose with conventional therapies. Holocaust survivors may have picked up fear from their ancestors and may be triggered into shock by something as innocuous as the mailman's loud knocking at the door. A man who seems to sabotage his life at every turn may be trying to pay back a brutal murder his great-grandfather committed. A brilliant lawyer who leaves his thriving practice to sail around the world and mysteriously disappears, never to be heard from again, might be resonating with his grandmother who was a lesbian and ostracized by the family

Honoring

The ties to our family and ancestors run deep. Even if we have estranged ourselves from our parents and ancestors or if they've died many years ago, the energetic cords may hold us as unwitting prisoners to them.

Honoring represents a level of awareness in itself. In the shamanic world, one might visit a certain location and pay respects to the nature spirits that reside there. To many, such a ritual may seem unnecessary and even ridiculous. But once you see that life is one, then honoring the spirit of the food you eat, the spirits of your ancestors, or the spirit of life, whether dead or alive, doesn't seem strange at all. Becoming one with life is paradoxical. Tibetan Buddhists call reality the void, which implies emptiness. However, the void is like a Grand Central Station teeming with life. There are many spirits and entities, an endless swirl of living energies that ultimately is one soul. Honoring is an elegant way of living, and honoring our ancestors may help untangle negative ties that subtly hold us back from surrender and awakening. Honoring can bring us a step closer to freedom.

Understanding Ancestral Karma

The ancestors and families we were born into represent the perfect conditions for our growth and are, in the deepest sense, the medicine that we need to grow. Constructing a detailed family tree, preferably going back at least three generations, helps to understand the genetic, geographic, and socioeconomic conditions of those who came before us. It sheds light on why these ancestors were right for us: why we needed to be part of a particular bloodline, and how it contributed to our lives.

Simply taking the time to construct the family tree is healing in itself because it begins to shed light on the unconscious level of shock that may be disturbing your energetic field. Answering the following questions can help to pinpoint the energetic crimps in the family soul:

Do you identify, or have a special connection with any particular relative or ancestor?

Do you or your family members observe that you are like one of your ancestors?

Do you know of any family secrets?

Have there been any abortions in your life? Has your mother or a grandmother had any abortions?

Are there any untimely or tragic deaths such as a stillbirth, the early loss of a sibling, suicide, or murder?

Are there any patterns of early death or illness in the family, such as cancer, heart disease, diabetes, arthritis, or paralysis?

Is there a pattern that occurs in chronological cycles such as accidents happening on birthdays or hitting a ceiling in relationships? (I know one man who has never had a girlfriend for longer than three dates.)

Any mental illness in the family?

Are there any patterns of addiction such as alcoholism or eating disorders?

Has an ancestor had an unusual fate?

Has any family member or ancestor been excluded or cast out from your family, such as a homosexual, one in prison, or a retarded child?

Are there financial issues such as great wealth, poverty, or fortunes made and lost? Was there any gain at the expense of others, such as in the case of slave ownership or theft?

What is the place of origin of your ancestors? What was the reason for and timing of their immigration if they immigrated to the United States or another country? Did they escape persecution or poverty?

Did you or anyone in your family serve in the military? Which wars and which battles?

What is your religious heritage? Do you practice your original religion or another? Are you estranged from your original religion? Are there any family members that have become nuns, monks, priests, or ascetics?

Is your home built on sacred ground, such as Native American burial grounds, or have you ever lived in a home built on sacred ground?

The Healer's Credo

As you go through these questions and build the family tree, try to understand what your ancestors and possibly your ancestors' victims may have gone through. However challenging the experiences they suffered, somehow use those challenges as a springboard to motivate yourself to live your life more fully. I call this attitude the Healer's Credo. If healers see suffering and pain, it doesn't make them bitter or depressed. On the contrary, it touches a chord in them that inspires to do the most they can to live and love more and to be on the side of healing.

Take for example two officers who survived a battle that cost the lives of many of the men in their charge. Initially, both men returned home deeply depressed. One of the officers became addicted to painkillers and couldn't work, and his health quickly went downhill. He admitted he felt as if he didn't deserve to live when so many under him had died. The other officer quickly snapped out of it. He also felt guilty and responsible, but he realized that if he went down with his men, he would only compound misery. If he accepted the reality of the tragedy—which couldn't be changed—and lived the best life possible, he would honor the men who died.

THE SPIRIT HOUSE

Nearly all ancient peoples understood the power of ancestral ties. The importance of ancestral harmony, even to the modern Chinese, is beautifully portrayed in the movie *Fearless*, with Jet Li. Jo Sen Ya is a skilled martial artist but a selfish man who cares only about fulfilling his ambition to be the best martial artist in China. He ends up killing a man in a fight. In retaliation, Jo's mother and young daughter are murdered. Deeply depressed, Jo leaves his home and travels to a faraway country province. He tries to commit suicide by drowning, but local people find him, and a young blind woman cares for him and falls in love with him. The beauty of the countryside and the simple warmth of the people heal Jo's heart. One day he hears some of the villagers talking about a ceremony to honor their ancestors, and Jo realizes that he must return to his city to visit the grave of his family. He leaves but promises the blind woman he will return.

Once in his home city, Jo goes to his ancestral tomb, bows down, and bares his heart and soul. He speaks to his parents and daughter as if they can hear every word. It is a turning point. Jo Sen Ya becomes clear on his life's purpose. While realizing his purpose, he is poisoned and dies, yet his desire to fulfill his promise to the blind woman is so strong that he returns to the countryside as a ghost for a last visit.

Many cultures the world over construct a place where the spirits of the departed ancestors may dwell. In Thailand, nearly every family has a spirit house. It is thought to provide stability in the spirit world. Spirit houses can be quite large, ornate, and beautiful. The living visit the spirit house and speak with their ancestors. They occasionally bring dishes of food or a sweet dessert that a particular family member enjoyed. Spirit houses can be as simple as a small shrine, perhaps with pictures, or whatever you'd like. Of course, the real shrine is the love and gratitude in your heart.

Past Lives: The Seedbed of Shock

Some say we pick our parents, and in a sense we do. The families we're born into are part of the mysterious order that works with each living being in the universe. Jesus referred to this omnipresent creative order when he said, "My father sees every sparrow fall." Native Americans call this order "The Great Mystery" because it seems to see into the deepest recesses of our heart and soul and reflect back to us the individual conditions we must pass through to experience growth and awakening. Call this power what you will, but the whole interacts with each of its parts in a mutually interdependent tapestry of undeniable perfection. Life gives us everything we need.

Samskaras is the Indian name given to the latent imprints we carry over from past lives. Generally, imprints come from uncompleted desires. If an old woman falls in love with painting and dies before she's actualized her art, her dying regret may be that she never became a competent artist. Perhaps next lifetime she's born into a family of artists where her love affair with painting can be fully realized. We always move toward the deepest desires of our heart and soul, and even death doesn't quench those desires. What can't be finished in one lifetime will be picked up again with a fresh body and renewed enthusiasm.

Of course, the imprints we carry from past lives may be negative. Unfinished anger, greed, or fear will compel us to be born again to complete it. Some meditation masters believe it may take lifetimes to work through even a single emotion. Supposedly, only when we have finished the journey through every state of consciousness, exhausted desire, and learned the significance of love will we escape the cycle of birth and death.

The Layering of Shock

Perhaps our past-life impressions attract us to a certain womb and family tree, which provides the exact conditions we need to grow. But along with it comes ancestral shock. Conception, pregnancy, and birth create fresh shock that fits tongue and groove with the areas we need to transform. Childhood wounds layer more shock on top of the deeper levels. The sum total of our shock makes up a large part of our ego identity: who we are and what we have to work with in this lifetime.

Shock Pools Together

From the deepest to the most superficial levels, shock is an energetic complex that spans the unconscious mind, the conscious mind, the energy body, and the physical body. Any of the encoded emotions, feelings, perceptions, smells, colors, images, or sounds may trigger latent shock. Each of the triggers is like a strand that connects to the center of a particular wound. And shock patterns may connect with other shock patterns like a great network of interconnected cobwebs. The mind tends to associate shock together as a collective pool.

Unconsciously, we mold our lives around shock, trying to protect ourselves from ever experiencing it again, and this control and manipulation run deeply through our lives.

We dream of living fully, of being adventurous and fearless, yet there's an unexplainable line, an unconscious aversion to enter into activities that may put us in the position of re-experiencing shock. Once badly burned, forever careful. That's why shock is the glue of the ego. It's so powerful that it instantly turns us inward into the safety and survival of the ego-self.

The trouble comes because no matter how carefully we try, we can't avoid becoming activated. Regardless of how long ago it happened, the shock pattern, with all its triggers, remains in the subconscious and unconscious mind. When the right strand is touched, one is back in shock, with its symptoms of fear, freezing, paralysis, and lack of clarity. When triggered, latent shock wounds send out mega-amplitude thought waves that jolt the sympathetic nervous system and crimp the flow of energy in our body. Instantly, we do what we've learned to do to survive: leave the body.

For many, the true self—the spark of conscious awareness—is like a hummingbird flitting inside a flower, but instead of finding nectar, a resting place of peace, it encounters broken glass and so flies quickly back out. This is happening continually. The Catch-22 is that we're not even aware of it. Sure, we often realize something's rough and jagged inside, but we've gotten used to it, compensated around it. This state of affairs has become so familiar it seems normal, and we've found coping mechanisms that make life tolerable.

Awakening: The Ultimate Healing

Until we get to the core and live from our real selves, we're like robots, always at the mercy of our deep unconscious programming. Some meditation masters insist that when we wake up, karma is absolved. If you think about it, the ramifications of unconscious shock are the deepest practical expression of what many call karma. When we get to the core of ourselves, we find the true being, the god within, the drop of the ocean, that which can't be touched, even by the unconscious. The real self lives in pure freedom. The absolute clarity of the self penetrates pre- and perinatal, ancestral, and past-life shock. The cycle of "the sins of the father are visited upon the sons" is broken. You stop unconsciously acting out your parents' roles and repeating your ancestral fate. You even see your past life impressions and have the choice of whether to continue with them.

Surrender and awakening allow us to acknowledge that all is as it has to be, even the horrific trials that you, your parents, your ancestors, and all of humanity struggle through. You understand the connections, like invisible, complex chords running through your ancestral tree. Your life, including the beauty and ugliness of your family history, becomes something that had to be, an unfailingly perfect order. You acknowledge your parents as vehicles, albeit imperfect ones. But no matter how much or how little we received from our biological parents, we're really children of life. Whatever struggles and resentment we may have had with our parents may be replaced with simple gratitude that they delivered us into the world; they gave us a body and, in many cases, material support. We wouldn't be who we are without them, or even be here.

But this can't be intellectual. Gratitude, forgiveness, or an opening of the heart can't be a concept. It has to be real, a non-ego forgiveness. If an ego forgives, that forgiveness is based on the ego being big enough to suspend its victimhood. If, however, you accept the entire package that life gave you because ultimately it's for your growth, you're not a victim at all. You're coming from a place of trusting life. It's a surrender, a letting go, and a hard corner in you liquefies and moves. Gratitude and understanding for life and its unwitting players untie the inner knots and disentangle you from your ancestors, parents, lovers, or others. Then the love circulates and flows again in your mind and body. You are no longer bound to your family in a destructive way. Acceptance, gratitude, and love allow you to transcend the family system. Native Americans say our true parents are Mother Earth and Father Sky. When you become a child of life and of your ancestors and your family, all of life secretly rejoices.

Suggestions for Practice:

On the road to surrender, it may help to honor your ancestors by constructing a family tree and making a spirit house.

Observing Past-life Shock

Latent shock from past lives fuels your deepest unconscious drives, but you don't have to experience past-life regressions or visit a psychic to know what those drives are. Whatever remains unfinished from your past lives will still be with you right now, in this lifetime. The best place to heal it is now, in the present. If you observe yourself carefully, you will be able to discern what your deepest drives and imprints are from past lives.

PART 6

Understanding Our Coping Mechanisms

Chapter 13

Shunting (Getting Away from the Mind)

In the last two chapters, we explored the origins, experience, and effects of shock. Now we'll look at the tricks and survival mechanisms the mind uses to protect itself from being overwhelmed by stress and shock.

This may be the most incredible time to live in the history of the world, but it comes with a price. The modern mind is frenetically active, spinning faster than ever before; it's gotten so used to being busy that our need to stay occupied is in the realm of sickness. According to a study by Cohen Children's Medical Center, the greatest cause of teen death in America—three thousand a year—is texting while driving. During a social event, such as a high school dance, some teens will sit against the wall texting, completely comfortable behind electronics, but not face-to-face with others or even with themselves. One may have thousands of friends on Facebook without really tasting life. We have more opportunities than ever, but we've lost ourselves in the process.

The intensity and sophistication of our entertainment reflects the increased chaos of the mind and a greater need to get away from ourselves. Even young children are hooked on computer and tablet games. In literature and cinema, there seems to be a trend toward larger-than-life themes. Look at the number of vigilante movies—huge muscle guys beating up and killing each other, with phenomenal special effects guaranteed to keep audience members on the edge of their seats for the entire film. When a famous Hollywood director was asked why he made such violent movies, he replied that those movies were what people wanted. If they weren't, society wouldn't support them, and, of course, that's true. The public demands ever-increasing intensity because the busy mind needs stronger and stronger stimuli to adequately occupy it.

The nature of the mind is to divide and separate the whole into parts. Like a computer search gone wild, the mind continually tries to find the answer. It reduces and chews up data until an answer is found. In this way, the mind is like a marvelous computer. Thinking to solve a problem may have positive aspects, such as in research, but the mind has become trained to constant busyness and doesn't know how to stop.

You've probably experienced this when you were trying to

remember something and it was just on the tip of your tongue but you couldn't pull it out. The mind doesn't give up easily. And unlike a computer that will tell you, "Nothing found, search over," when there is no answer, the mind continues to work. It can't sit in silence for more than a few seconds without getting nervous. It needs to stay occupied nearly all the time. If it doesn't have a problem to solve or a task to do, it will create one.

Try eating breakfast with nothing to do—no computer, tablet, or phone. The mind jumps from looking at the cereal box or the mail to looking around the room for something, anything, to occupy itself. It will ponder, free-associate, or even carry on a conversation with itself. Busyness such as this is so normal that we take it for granted, but as you get deeper into the observation process, you'll see it's actually an annoyance that steals your peace, a mosquito that keeps biting at your nervous system.

The double negative of the mind is that it must be busy, but the same busyness causes stress, hence the need to distract the mind from itself. Shunting might be likened to the fan on your computer. When there's too much activity, heat is produced and the fan switches on to cool things down. Similarly, when the mind reaches a certain degree of discomfort, experiencing stress, anxiety, or boredom, we shunt away. Another expression of shunting might be using a comfort-seeking device—and we all have them.

Concentrating on some distasteful chore, such as preparing taxes, one seems unable to resist the pull of checking e-mail, getting up, listening to a song, or texting a friend. If you were a fly on the wall watching yourself, you'd seem to be jumping around like an erratic puppet, and guess who's the puppet master holding the strings? The mind, of course. What's really happening with shunting is that the mind takes a break and checks out to avoid feeling inner anxiety. Shunting is a normal way to occupy the mind, and certainly not bad. It's a pleasure to watch a movie, read a book, or take a break to get away from ourselves. But shunting is also often unconscious. Productivity coaches tell us that shunting is an enemy and that we have to train ourselves to focus; but more important, shunting is another way in which we lose awareness. And in our practice, we don't want to unconsciously shunt away from anything that's going on inside us.

In Jack London's *White Fang*, an old Native American man takes a liking to a young white boy and tries to help him find himself. The old man tells the boy that if he can't sit in silence for an hour without doing anything, there is little hope for him. The mind's very nature is movement; it must do something, needs occupation. The inner self, however, rejoices in stillness and silence. Few in modern society can simply sit in stillness with nothing to do. (The ability to do so implies going through the same inner process outlined in this book.)

Suggestions for Practice

Sit and Do Nothing

Sit quietly with nothing to do. Observe how long the mind will let you simply sit in peace without piping in or looking for something to occupy it. Notice that even positive thoughts or fantasies create movement and activate the nervous system, thereby stealing peace.

Waiting in Peace

Spending the first thirty-three years of my life in New York, I noticed how impatient people became waiting in line. If the cashier was slow for any reason, you could feel the tension in the room like a coiled spring. People kept glancing at their watches, itching to move on to the next task, their minds racing ahead. I commonly heard sighs, curses, and comments. Next time this happens to you, instead of being like a greyhound at the gate or trying to distract yourself, try completely letting go of the mind and resting in the true self. Relax every muscle and nerve in the body and feel the energy circulating in the body. Waiting with the true self transforms tension into rejuvenation.

Observe How You Shunt

Be aware of the ways you shunt. Most of them are unconscious habits. See if, before you shunt, you can be aware of the trigger. This is similar to the practice of meditation, where one tries to sit without moving a muscle. While meditating, the urge to move or scratch may arise. It's amusing to try to watch your process unfold. Normally, the mind gives a subconscious command to move and you follow through without conscious awareness. Watching your entire process brings the subconscious trigger to the conscious mind. You watch but don't give in to the trigger, and eventually the itch or need to move dissipates like smoke. If you must move, at least do it consciously. This is another way to see how we jump to the dictates of the mind without even knowing it. But our practice is obviously not confined to the cushion. Your clear consciousness watches your mind throughout the entire day.

Chapter 14

Dark Meditation

IF SHUNTING IS LIKE A FAN USED TO COOL DOWN AN OVER-heated mind, dark meditation is a survival mechanism. It's the ultimate vehicle of distraction. I call it dark not because it's evil but because it's the flip side of true meditation. With dark meditation just as with true meditation, one goes into a state of no mind.

Owning Mahoney, a documentary about gambling addiction, is a remarkable portrayal of the total occupation that dark meditation provides. Mahoney, an investment banker, is addicted to gambling and even embezzles his clients' money to pay for his habit. He sits at the Las Vegas tables until they close, without eating or drinking and barely moving. When many hours later the tables finally close, it's as if he's waking from a daze. He can't believe the time has passed so quickly; it had seemed like mere minutes.

Losing the Self

Dark meditations, unlike the use of comfort-seeking devices, are not ordinary habits. The hallmark of dark meditation is the total loss of self. They are terribly alluring and the mind becomes completely absorbed in the activity. The particular vehicle one chooses fits tongue and groove with one's psyche. If food has the power to completely engross the conscious mind, thereby distracting the unconscious, one turns to eating. Drugs, shopping, alcohol, sex, or gambling might be the dark meditation for another. The demarcating line between dark and true meditation is the quality of consciousness; therefore, even a positive activity could function as a dark meditation, such as exercise or obsessing that the house, yard, or car be perfect. Even prayer can be a dark meditation if it is mindless distraction from inner pain.

True meditation is beneficial because awareness and receptivity are present—you're in the body. Circulation opens, which provides feelings of bliss and an increase of energy and clarity. With dark meditation, clear awareness is numbed and accompanied by an outward movement of consciousness from the body. Dark meditation, though it offers a similar break from our minds as true meditation—and may feel good while we do it—fails to leave one refreshed or feeling centered. One usually feels keyed up, unbalanced, and off center because inner tension inhibits the flow of circulation. The bottom line with dark meditation is that one is not here—not at home in the body.

Dark Meditation: A Mental Antidote to Shock

The mind lives on a merry-go-round ride of desire and fear. We desire pleasure and fear pain, but they are opposite sides of the same coin. When we reach the zenith of pain, it may turn to pleasure, and when pleasure reaches its height, the pendulum swings and may turn to pain. It seems crazy that people sometimes take pleasure in pain and that pleasure can be painful, but this is merely the duality of emotion. You see this pendulum-swinging cycle in dark meditation.

Because shock is the greatest terror, pain, and discomfort, the vehicle used for the dark meditation must be the counterpoint: the opposite side of the pendulum. Dark meditations are usually extraordinarily compelling desires that have the power to distract us from our particular shock. In a sense, we create an antidote, a habit, a counter-wrinkle in our mind that's compelling enough to distract us from the internal pressure of shock. For this reason, dark meditation frequently turns to addiction.

Dark Meditation as Addiction

People say a stoner loves his drugs, but many times he doesn't love his addiction at all. It's the absolute need to get away from shock that compels one to turn to drugs again and again. One must distract oneself from overwhelming feelings at all costs. Especially when triggered, or just about to be, one will turn to one's particular dark meditation. Shock, therefore, is the most important factor behind all addictive practices.

I knew a woman who used suicide attempts as her dark meditation. When her shock was triggered, she'd take sleeping pills or cut her wrists. She obviously didn't want to die; she always made sure someone found her in time to bring her to the hospital. The psych ward would keep her for a few days to a week and, until she was released, she had a break, a distraction from her normal routine and lots of attention. Her psychiatrist cautioned that she must be closely watched. Attempting suicide had been established as a pattern in her consciousness. If life got rough, she'd do it again.

Dark meditation takes root in the body, the brain, and the nervous system, and these roots run very deep. You can cut down the tree with willpower, but the roots remain. Feed it, even a little bit, and the dark meditation can sprout anew. If you turn to that dark meditation, you will lose yourself. Whether it's for a half hour, a month, or a lifetime, you will lose yourself. Once one becomes enmeshed with a particular dark meditation, dabbling is not possible. One always lands right back in the thick of the addiction.

I once knew a man who held a responsible, steady job for fifty years. On his annual two-week vacation, he took a hotel room alone and got super-drunk. When the two weeks had passed, he'd sober up and go back to work. For fifty years he gave himself only two weeks a year for his dark meditation, but those two weeks created a complete hole in his memory. That's why Alcoholics Anonymous insists that an alcoholic remains an alcoholic, even after thirty years of sobriety. Once the dark meditation has been deeply established in the mind and the nervous system as your antidote to shock, it's always waiting, and once restarted, it will be as if you'd never left.

Dark Meditation and Your Health

Some habits are obviously more harmful than others, but most if not all dark meditations agitate the nervous system and take a toll on health.

Yoga and Ayurveda speak of the three *gunas*, or qualities of life. *Sattva* is pure, blissful, constructive energy, *raja* is stimulation and action, and *tamas* is inertia. It's a common misconception that a yogi or sage attains total *sattva*, or a pure state of existence. It may be that *sattva* becomes the sage's primary energy, but action, rest, and bliss are all part of life. In healthy individuals the *gunas* are in balance. You might say that bliss arises when stimulation and rest (yin/yang) are in perfect balance. Buddha described this as the middle way. Precisely between yin and yang lies balance and ecstasy; one sees the reality of life and is content.

Dark meditations create imbalance. They are invariably stimulating (*rajasic*) and affect sleep and the ability to deeply rest. They often change one's eating habits. They take a toll on the body and necessitate a swing of the pendulum toward *tamas*: inertia. Imbalances in *tamas* and *raja* activate the nervous system, contentment vanishes, and one becomes more prone to disease.

I've used heart-rate variability (HRV) testing to illustrate this difference between balance and imbalance. HRV is the physiological phenomenon of variation in the time interval between heartbeats. If a healthy woman had a pulse rate of sixty beats per minute, one would assume that her heart would beat exactly once a second. Yet the opposite is true. In a healthy person, there are minute variabilities in the way the heart beats. The more variability in the heartbeat, the more fluid and healthy she is. HRV is helpful in determining physical and emotional health because it is an accurate measure of the autonomic nervous system.

I've taken baseline HRT readings with patients and then tested them while they engaged in their dark meditation. A thirty-eight-year-old male was tested standing and lying down. His basic health was measured on a scale of 1.1-13.7, the lower number numbers being more favorable. His average score after ten trials was 7.3. After being engaged in his dark meditation—Internet poker—for thirty minutes, his average health score was 9.7, also measured on ten separate occasions.

However, it's rather foolish to tell someone he'd be better off without his dark meditations. Even the most unconscious addicts know their habit isn't good for them, but they can't seem to stop. It seems a mystery—why would anyone willingly injure himself? The degree to which one's mind is torturing him determines his need to distract himself from it.

Piercing Dark Meditations

Before we begin, let's drop the good and bad labels about our habits. They have served us—as a counterbalance, a form of protection, and a survival mechanism. In Japan it is said that our imperfections are part of an overall perfection. Similarly, dark meditations make one distinctly human. Frequently, people who rigidly repress their dark habits become so holier than thou that they also become impossible to live with, or perhaps much worse. Many so-called "perfect" people are deeply ill, fanatical, sadistic, and masochistic. Adolf Hitler was said to be an extraordinarily disciplined man. He didn't drink, smoke, or womanize. He was a strict vegetarian. Hitler, like many in religious orders, considered himself to be righteous and superior to the weaker man who gives in to his indulgence. Some theorize that if Hitler had used alcohol or had a weakness for women or some other vice, he would have been a softer, humbler man and may never have unleashed such a destructive force of anger and hatred on the planet.

I'm not sure if anything is completely bad or good. Stan Grof, MD, has shown that drugs such as LSD and even ecstasy can be of tremendous help to people. Marijuana, once propagandized as evil, is now being used by millions for chronic pain and appears to be a potential cure for certain cancers. Beer, wine, alcohol, coffee, tea, and chocolate, once thought to be health destroyers, are now known to have certain health benefits. Rather than being ashamed of your dark meditations, I suggest you respect them as part of your individual perfection, and as a personal vehicle for growth.

Sometimes, remaining in the clutches of addiction can be fatal. In such cases, the habit must be stopped to save lives. However, if one's particular dark meditation isn't going to severely harm him or anyone else, it doesn't have to be repressed with willpower. This is far better, as repressing or trying to cut out dark meditations without dealing with the underlying shock may backfire and cause a deeper problem. Down the line, one might end up expressing a dark meditation in a more harmful manner, such as a celibate priest who represses his sexuality and abuses children or women in his congregation. Rather than repressing, it's best to start by being natural—by accepting exactly who and what we are, and trusting that life has us under its wing. If your particular dark meditation isn't life-threatening or overly dangerous to anyone's well-being, just let it be, without judgment. Give yourself permission to explore it more deeply.

Things to Observe about the Dark Meditation

Don't judge with your mind or by any moral or ethical ideal. Watch with the eyes of your heart and soul and ask yourself these six questions:

Do you lose yourself?

How much time does it take?

Does it serve your life?

Are you betraying your own life?

Does it provide freedom or bondage?

Are you addicted to chaos?

Losing the Self

To what degree did you lose yourself?

Dark meditations change people. The habit takes over the person. Loss of self means one isn't all there, so one isn't quite in balance or centered, and this off-centeredness might spill over into one's life. One might make small but costly mistakes, such as when driving a car. One might be quicker to become annoyed or angry or may have a lower frustration or overwhelm point. Frequently, the more overwhelmed one gets, the more one turns to the dark meditation.

Losing Time

How much time do you spend on your dark meditation?

When you lose yourself in a dark meditation, the hands of the clock spin, the day passes. Necessary things get neglected and fall by the wayside. Chores don't get done, paperwork piles up, kids don't get played with. Frustration builds. The mind becomes more heated and you get even more paralyzed into shock. It becomes a vicious cycle.

A woman came to me and said with obvious embarrassment, "There's nothing wrong with what I'm doing."

"What is it?" I asked.

"I look at fashion on the Internet. There's nothing wrong in it."

"Then why are you telling me about it?"

"Well, I spend hours with it. The day passes and I've probably looked at clothes, makeup, and jewelry for four or five hours. I can't stop. Nothing gets done."

"Seeing this is excellent," I said. "Now watch every bit of it more carefully."

Dark meditations are usually extraordinarily private, even when performed with another. They separate one into the ego completely and affect how much time one has for other people. They can even replace relationships.

A young couple came to me because the husband wasn't able to have an erection.

"Well, it's no mystery," his wife said. "He looks at porn all evening."

"Hey, I'm a guy," the man said. "I love sex. Looking at a little porn is natural."

I ran a male hormone profile and his testosterone was off-the-charts low. Previously, his testosterone count had been normal, but the constant mental stimulation from porn had depleted his hormones to the point where he was incapable of having sex with his wife, who was quite an attractive woman.

That doesn't seem like the desired outcome for a man who loves sex, but with dark meditations, the mind takes a normal need and twists it into something gone wild. We all need to eat—and by all means, enjoy it to the fullest. But when food goes to the mind, it becomes a disorder, a sickness way beyond our bodily needs. Sex is natural, but when it goes to the mind it becomes insatiable. No matter how much one has, it's not enough. When a normal need enters the mind, it becomes larger than life. The mind can never get enough of the dark meditation. It will cleverly rationalize and devise ways to continue the dark meditation, as with the religious alcoholic who convinces himself he's going to the bar to save some souls and has to have a couple of drinks just to fit in. Remember, the mind can rationalize anything we do. *I work so hard. I deserve a treat. I earned this.* The mind plays endless tricks that are well worth watching.

Does It Serve Your Life?

When I was young, my goal was to start a healing retreat center. One of the meditation masters with whom I'd studied not only had created a large ashram, which was his headquarters, but had also had a thousand-acre retreat center in northern California. I wondered how he, and others like him, were able to manifest their dreams so successfully.

A large part of their success is the strength of their focus. In Chapter 10, we spoke of the vision that burns in the heart and helps to guide us through life. A meditation master is so clear that her focus is a shining beacon that rarely gets interrupted. Most of us, even if we do have a vision, don't have the same laser-like power of clarity. Our focus is more like a flickering light bulb. We give a little energy to our vision, become distracted, and then go back again intermittently. In the case of dark meditations, we completely lose ourselves.

How does the complete interruption of clarity, focus, and awareness affect the manifestation of your visions?

Making the World a Better Place

A byproduct of opening the heart is increased awareness and compassion for the tremendous pain and suffering of the world. But how do we help alleviate it? Some meditation masters have suggested that the only way to really help others is the inner way: to awaken and help others to awaken. When a person awakens, that moment is said to have an uplifting effect on all of life. The consciousness of the whole is raised. The external way to ease suffering is by helping and serving others. Since life is one soul, it really doesn't matter how one serves, but there's one necessary element: awareness. You have to be present to help anyone.

How do dark meditations fit in with your desire to make the world a better place?

Are You Betraying Your Own Life?

It's far more common to betray ourselves than to be betrayed by another. If my partner stole money from our business, I can blame him, but it might be more real and productive to look at me. Why did I believe in an untrustworthy man? Was there some greed or laziness on my part that allowed or set up his actions?

If my wife has a relationship with another man, it may appear as if she betrayed me. After all, I'd been faithful. On the surface, I'd done everything that a good partner was supposed to do. But things aren't always what they seem. Maybe I didn't allow her to be herself. Perhaps I controlled her or stifled her growth, or maybe I just stopped growing years ago. On paper it seems as if she betrayed me, but actually I may have betrayed her and therefore us. For her own growth she was compelled to look elsewhere. Her actions might even be praiseworthy. She had the courage to end a relationship that wasn't serving either of us. Because she didn't betray herself, we both have a fresh chance to grow. Even if someone actually does betray me, I have to ask if I'm betraying myself by holding on to it. Life is too deep to neatly figure it all out, but don't look to how others have hurt you. Look more to how you betray your own life by injuring your growth or freedom.

How Do You Tell If You Are Betraying Yourself?

Each of us is a delicate balance of physical, mental, emotional, unconscious, and spiritual. Many things can throw a wrench into our inner well-being. The yardstick for measuring whether something brings you freedom is how much tension it creates inside you. When you go against the grain of your heart and soul, you will feel it in your body via the nervous system. Simply observe how you feel. There's no way to fool yourself. You can try, but the internal feeling that you're violating your own heart and soul will continue.

Don't try to be a perfect Muslim, Christian, Buddhist, Hindu, or Jew. Seek your own perfection, which means to be disentangled, unburdened, content, and truly at peace within your own skin. Perfection comes when you stop the internal conflict inside yourself so that you are free. The true self settles and takes root in an unburdened body so it can enjoy life as it is. The mind, on the other hand, thrives on conflict, and so the battle begins.

The Inner Battle

When people ask me to help them cut out a habit, they are usually fed up. There's a predictable cycle: they want to stop, but they continually turn to the habit. They beat themselves up, promise never to do it, but fail again and again, damaging self-esteem and confidence.

When I was a teenager, I smoked pot without a trace of guilt. But after getting seriously into kung fu, a strange worm crept into my normally carefree attitude around getting high. I felt as if I were building myself up on one hand through intense workouts, yoga, and meditation, and sabotaging myself on the other. I continued with the pot for a while, but the vibration just didn't mix anymore. Every time I smoked, I felt off. I knew deep inside that marijuana was no longer serving me; it was a contradiction, and the pressure on my nervous system was tremendous. This contradiction escalated to a war inside me, and my body became the battlefield.

There's no need to buy into the guilt trips that society, religion, or family lay on us, but there's a type of guilt that should be heeded: the unique feeling we get when we violate our own selves. What does this mean? When you begin to awaken, you simply can't go unconscious anymore. Your inner self doesn't want to go back to sleep, so it screams at you. Eventually, the pleasure I received from getting high was outweighed by the internal conflict I was experiencing. At that point, smoking pot dropped away without any effort, repression, or willpower on my part. It just let go by itself.

Non-effort is the method of spirit. On the highest level, there's nothing to be done. It all happens by itself. Even within effort, non-effort can be observed throughout the entire awakening process. The inner flame is lighted and life prepares you from the inside out. There are no mental decisions. Nothing is violently cut out of you. It all happens in the interphase between the real and the false selves. The more aware one becomes, the more obvious it is: the dark meditation creates inner discord. If you refuse to listen to your inner self, you will continue to wreak havoc within yourself.

Resist Not Evil

Buddha said one should keep a pure mind. This statement has been misconstrued to mean a clean mind: chaste and proper. The real meaning is a *still* mind. Buddha wasn't saying one should think only good thoughts. He meant *no thought*. All thoughts are impure because they are impediments that keep us from awakening. When Christ said resist not evil, he meant the same thing Buddha meant: all thoughts obstruct the purity of no mind. The mind, our trusted confidant, is the evil that Christ referred to.

But don't fight (resist) the mind; just let it be. Watch it without judgment. When the flame of the inner self (consciousness) is hot enough, it effortlessly burns away what's no longer needed. Whatever the flame doesn't consume must still be needed, in the sense that tension is still required to get to surrender.

Freedom

After I stopped smoking pot, I was surprised how relieved I felt. I'd never really paid attention to how much had been involved in the habit. First I had to spend the time to go to a dealer to buy pot—not to mention that marijuana was illegal and getting busted for even small amounts was possible. Then I had to clean the pot and roll it into cigarettes. After smoking I used breath mints and some sort of cologne, and I put drops in my eyes to take the red out. When I stopped using pot, I felt great freedom. I didn't have to bother with it anymore. One fewer entanglement to weigh me down. The cycle of bondage had been broken.

Are You Addicted to the Cycle of Chaos?

A surprising number of people are more comfortable in turmoil and chaos than they are with freedom and peace.

For many, chaos has been the normal state of affairs for a long time and they've grown addicted to the tension even though it's a vicious circle of self-sabotage. Chaos makes the ego stronger because there is a problem to solve, but being addicted to chaos is bondage. When a person wakes up, the addiction to chaos ends. One ceases to fight, even with oneself. Whatever is causing inner tension and slavery is naturally discarded, be it a job, a relationship, a habit, bad blood, or a way of thinking.

Not Telling You to Stop

Nor am I giving you permission to continue with them. I suggest meditating on the six questions above only to increase clarity and awareness, which often leads to a quickening of the friction point: the interphase between the real and false selves. This interphase is where the inner battle and transformation occur.

I sometimes wonder about those who've never tasted their dark sides. Some of the yoga masters who came to America in the sixties and seventies claimed to be celibates, but when they came face-to-face with adoring female students who weren't sexually inhibited in the least, some of them found themselves in water too deep to handle. These masters thought they had transformed their sexuality, but they'd never explored it—only repressed it.

It seems that the real master knows both sides. He has tasted the dark and transformed it into light, but the darkness has not been banished; he carries it within him as power. The inner battle marinates; the struggle breeds wisdom. The dark meditation has a distinct purpose. How does one become seasoned in anything? Through experience and observation of that experience.

Be careful what you ask for, especially awakening. The more the inner self wakes up, the more aware you are and the more sensitive you will become. Things you'd been able to do without a flicker of tension before might cause discomfort as your inner eyes open. You become more aware of reality, so the conflict caused by dark meditations becomes more obvious.

Unless your dark meditation is life-threatening, there's no hurry or need to stop. The fruit will ripen when it's ready. If the roots of desire run deeply, we must pass through the whole gamut of the dark meditation and experience its full effect. When the real self takes the captain's seat, we no longer need to distract ourselves from ourselves, and the dark meditation lets go all by itself. But if it's not time, don't force it. Don't be violent with your dark meditation or yourself. It just leads to taking yourself too seriously. If, for now, you've looked at the dark meditation with your heart and soul and still want to continue, drop the resistance to it.

A man came to me because he smoked a few cigarettes a day. He tortured himself over it because smoking wasn't good for his health. Everyone knows smoking isn't good for the body, but in a case such as this, it's possible that the mental unrest and self-degradation—the inner chaos—outweigh the damage that smoking a couple of cigarettes might cause. Some dark meditations may accompany this particular body and mind to the grave.

The bottom line is stopping the inner war one way or another. Only you can decide which way provides greater freedom. Either accept that your dark meditation is part of your life, at least for now, or let go of it. Always be kind to yourself as you explore dark meditations.

Suggestions for Practice

Make Dark Meditation a Ceremony

Amp up awareness and go as deeply as you can into your dark meditations. Because dark meditations are attempts at neutralizing shock, the very hallmark is unconsciousness. One automatically slips into the robotic habit that he or she is trained into. But now try to make the entire process more conscious. Be a fly on the wall watching yourself. Be aware of every nuance of the habit.

In general, watch the total effect your particular dark meditation has on you, including when you're not doing it. Notice how it occupies your thoughts and how you manage your life around it. Observe your state of mind when the desire to do it arises, such as when a smoker has the desire to light up after a meal.

The trigger to shock is often unconscious and so subtle that one doesn't know he is internally overwhelmed and about to turn to a dark meditation. But if you are aware, the unconscious signal to go into a dark meditation is almost like the prodrome (early symptom) of a migraine sufferer. It can be witnessed.

During any dark meditation, watch how quickly you go into complete absorption. Try to retain the witness, even for a few seconds. Notice how you want to forget awareness and slip into unconsciousness. Mindless unconsciousness is what you long for, but try to keep consciousness present for as long as possible. If you can retain awareness, you'll see that the real self is not attracted to or affected by the dark meditation at all. It has no interest whatsoever. The mind is pulling so strongly because it wants to be occupied and, on a deeper level, craves busyness and conflict. Watch the pull of the mind. It's only a voice from the false self but a very powerful one.

Try to notice your breathing and how you feel during the dark meditation. Usually one is tense and barely breathing, which reflects the state of the nervous system. Where is clear consciousness? Gone, of course. The dark meditation is totally occupying the mind. Your real self is not home. Afterward, be aware of the ramifications. How do you feel immediately after? Do you sleep well? And how do you feel the following day? Ponder the six questions covered in this chapter.

PART 7

Piercing Shock

Chapter 15

The Secret Place of the Most High

THE STATUS-QUO DOCTOR OR THERAPIST WORKS IN THE realm of replacement therapy. It's actually quite easy to replace one habit with a less destructive one because the mind is so malleable and trainable. If you stop a dangerous activity and begin a positive or less harmful one, the mind latches on to the new one. If you keep repeating it, a new wrinkle forms in the mind. In twenty-one days, nearly any habit can be replaced. I've seen this with many alcoholics, who might give up drink but turn to smoking cigarettes or drinking pots of coffee.

Switching to a less damaging obsession is considered positive, and when one can replace a destructive habit with something beneficial, it's considered a great success. If yoga replaces an eating disorder, or meditation takes the place of drugs, certainly it's an improvement to one's life and health, yet the inner mind remains the same. It's only a new obsession—albeit a positive one—that's taken over the job of distraction. When I was young, I traded my drug habit for martial arts, meditation, and yoga. When my shock surfaced, I used them to distract. If I felt uncomfortable, I had something to do: work out, sit in meditation, or regulate my breath until I felt better. But until I got to the core, ultimately I was still repressing the shock. It remained deep inside—untouched—waiting to be activated.

Distracting ourselves from shock never solves the true inner tension, for the obvious reason that shock—the very glue of the ego—is merely pushed away and buried. The burglar in the basement remains.

Repression for the Majority

As B.K.S. Iyengar said: "Only when your inner self sees what eclipses itself, can you experience true freedom." But that revelation is not common knowledge or else many more people would be living in freedom. It's difficult to make the leap, because the psyche protects itself. You have to allow yourself to go into and get to know the shock, and this surrender is a deep phenomenon. One must be willing to experience deep elemental fear. The psyche, however, has been built on pleasure and pain. It wants to keep the pleasurable activities, hold on to them, and experience them again and again—forever, if possible. On the other hand, the psyche prefers to cut out whatever causes us pain and fear. But if we can't cut it away no matter how hard we try, we attempt to push it away. Pushed into the basement, the shock remains, waiting for the right trigger to become activated.

Severely shocked individuals may never possess the inner strength to walk through the valley of death. The fear involved with facing their elemental shock would be too great. To get to the core is for the relatively few because, ultimately, one has to re-experience shock. Few actually want to face themselves at such an uncomfortable level. I've lost patients by telling them to stop getting away from their depression and, instead, get into it. Immersing oneself in pain can be too scary a place to be. They've spent their lives doing everything possible to escape it. But piercing our demons and entering, open-eyed, into shock is not only the most efficient way to transform shock but also a bridge to awakening. Realizing that your deepest fears are not real is a huge step in becoming free.

To penetrate shock, you must develop the presence of your inner self to the extent that you can reverse the natural impulse for your consciousness to flee and instead bring awareness right inside the center of the emotion. It's enormously difficult to do so, because the escape mechanism has become hardwired into the nervous system. Activation into shock is unconscious. It happens like a knee-jerk reaction, just as fast as thought. Many times you aren't even aware that a trigger has been touched, but something happens inside: a change in blood sugar, a pain, a sensation, an unknown thought, seeing a certain color. You've brushed a delicate strand of the shock wound and you're gone, out of the body and floundering to regain comfort.

The first step is to become aware that consciousness has been lost. But this step is difficult because the very nature of shock is so intense and overwhelming that one is often too caught up in fear to be aware of anything. Even after you develop the presence to know what's happening, the immediate or impending terror and discomfort of shock and the subsequent mega-high-amplitude thought waves clamp down on the nervous system, which keeps consciousness moving toward the exit ramp. External coping methods of controlling shock, such as putting hot and cold packs on your hands, head, or neck, are only bandages to calm you down. Developing the knack for immediately bringing consciousness back to the body is the key. You don't necessarily want to calm yourself down externally; rather, learn to bring clear awareness right into the center of the emotion or else you may miss a golden opportunity.

What's inside your own mind is the most terrifying thing you will ever experience. But it isn't a thought that causes pain; rather, it's the emotional reaction to thought, or aftershock. When the unseen trigger is tripped, one immediately goes into a manifestation of shock and generally leaves the body.

The trail that leads to your core, therefore, isn't traveled through thought, analysis, learning the original cause of the wound, integrating your inner child, or playing any such mind games whatsoever. Using the ego mind to cure itself is impossible, but it's so tempting to try because the nature of the mind is to want to know the answer. Avoid that trap, as it never works. It's the feeling—in the body—that must be entered into. *A Course in Miracles* makes the case that love and fear are the only true emotions. But enter your emotion in whatever form it presents: depression, grief, apathy, unworthiness, anger, frustration, or deep fear. The trick is to go completely into the emotion. It takes inner muscles you never knew existed to hold your consciousness inside the feeling. The effort of staying in the body might even make you tremble.

A Switch of Polarities

Up until this point, you may have used some sort of effort in searching for the true self, observing the mind, and practicing holding yourself in the body, even during fear or shock. But once in the center of the emotion, you completely surrender. If you stay with it, you'll get deeper and deeper into a place, much like entering the eye of a hurricane. All around, emotion rages like a wild tempest. If you lose awareness, you can easily become activated and fly out of the body. If you hold the true self at the core, you'll feel energy swirling around you, but inside you will be perfectly quiet. This is the very center—what some have called the secret place of the most high, the abode of soul, or the god within. Nothing can touch you here; you are in great peace. And from this place, you (the real self) see that shock isn't real. Even our greatest terror is merely an old, deeply ingrained pattern that has absolutely no substance. As soon as the inner eyes see, the hooks of the shock disentangle from your consciousness. Once you—the *real* you—have witnessed from the secret place of the most high, you'll never be quite the same. You've created separation from your shock.

In finding the secret place of the most high, you'll have passed through the demons of the mind and found the absolute core of you. It doesn't mean you'll never experience fear or shock again—the same energetic triggers may be activated—but you'll know what's happening and how to bring your true self back to the core. You'll know that shock isn't quite real; it's just another old story, and having no substance, it ultimately can't touch you. Identification with the shock is interrupted, and any fear, worry, or strong feeling can be penetrated this way. Once you have reached the center, you'll be able to access the secret place of the most high more easily. It's a huge step.

Suggestions for Practice

Entering Shock

Entering shock is not remembering or conjuring up an old feeling. When activated, you'll find yourself right back in the original shock. One may experience abject terror, feel paralyzed, or be incoherent. I've seen people enter so deeply into shock that they don't know who they are or where they are. Many regress to the age when they first experienced shock. I've seen elderly people go back to their childhood and even their birth. It can be quite overwhelming.

Penetrating your shock through observation can take time. It may take years of gradually testing the waters. Don't approach shock with a macho attitude, as if the more you can take the better. When shock is severe, let yourself experience a tiny bit at a time. As you approach severe shock, experience the feeling for even a few seconds and then come out again. There is really no need to look for shock; when you are ready, it will certainly find you. When it does, don't push it away or hide from it, but also don't fight with it or force anything. Just keep awareness. As you surrender, it's possible to start to freeze and lose awareness, but be natural and just observe; continue to bring your clear consciousness into the feeling as a witness.

Staying in the Body

Dark meditations and the underlying shock propel us from the body and therefore effectively block our journey to our core. It's a continual strengthening of the inner self's presence that prepares you to penetrate your deepest shock, which is why there can really never be shortcuts. The practice of being aware of when your consciousness is in the body, and when it gets derailed, is crucial. As you go about the day, try to keep your inner self in the body as much as possible. When you find yourself in the mind, bring your true self back.

You can try to devise a method to remind yourself to amp up your awareness of the real self, such as setting an alarm on your watch, but the only true method is your sincerity. When your inner being is on fire, the presence of the real self stays focused.

Sitting in Shock

When you're more familiar with shock, keep bringing awareness back inside you and try to sit with whatever is going on there, right in the feeling. If you wake up at night—and things always seem darkest in the middle of the night—try to sit in the very center of the emotion, whatever it is. As difficult as it may be, let the witness fully experience the feeling as much as possible. Bring yourself to the core of the pain and surrender completely. It's never the analysis of thoughts or going back to the cause but surrendering deeply into the emotion with full awareness that leads you to the secret place of the most high.

Chapter 16

Rites of Passage (The External Approach)

MANY PEOPLE HAVE ASKED ME HOW THEY CAN CUT OUT their fear, but if you were to cut out any part of yourself, you wouldn't be whole or who you are meant to be. Fear itself is ancient. It's transferred from the misty beginnings of human existence, and it's in nearly everyone in one form or another. One might be brave enough to fight in the ring but terrified of love. One might have the courage to walk a tightrope two hundred feet above a chasm but be afraid of snakes. Some are afraid of not being seen, others of being seen. Some tell you not to be afraid, but fear and shock aren't the enemy. *The integration and transformation of fear is probably the ultimate portal to growth.*

The previous chapter took the approach of piercing shock internally. You can't skip that part. Going inside develops the inner presence to enter shock, find the core, and ultimately surrender. The outer road of piercing fear and shock is merely the other side of the coin, and life always embraces all sides. There are times you need to go out to get in. To realize your dreams, first pass through shock internally and then complete the act externally. This may be called a "rite of passage."

Traditional Rites of Passage

Rites of passage were a crucial part of many older cultures. When young people came of age, during the difficult time of puberty and before marriage, they were often put in isolation to face themselves through a hardship: perhaps a dangerous hunt, a long fast, or a ritual of some kind. But the most difficult and profound aspect of any rite of passage is going into your own mind. Perhaps the young questers came into contact with the alive part of them, their true being. During the process, a vision might surface to give a quester insight on how to live his or her life. Such rites have been almost completely overlooked in modern society, which is why so many people are still looking for themselves, no matter what their age.

Contemporary Rites of Passage

Have you ever seen an overweight, out-of-shape person on an army-style obstacle course? Maybe she's sweating and her muscles are straining and trembling, yet her face shines with triumph. She looks very alive. Contemporary rites of passage push people to go beyond what they thought they could do. Self-help seminars and business retreats often include some modern form of rite of passage because they take people out of their comfort zones and show them they're capable of much more than they realized. Passing through fear and going beyond it can enrich a person long after the event is over.

Personal Rites of Passage

A personal rite of passage is self-directed. No one urges you to embark on it. There's no obstacle course, no group cheering you on. If you're afraid of water, no one coaches you to get into the pool. Certain fears or phobias need not be entered into. What does it matter if you're afraid of mice? How is it holding you back from living? It's a mere quirk of your psyche.

Personal rites of passage resolve the internal conflicts that *do* prevent you from living. You pass through what you *know* is holding you back. Your being intuitively knows that passing through a particular blockage is a crossroads and an opportunity. If you push away the inner conflict, you may avoid discomfort, but the burglar remains in the basement. There's clarity; your inner voice is screaming, almost like a broadcast from your deathbed. If you don't pass through this obstacle, you're missing an opportunity to live.

There may be anticipation around a rite of passage. If you have shock around performance, you might feel anxiety as soon as you make the arrangements to perform. You can expect this when you face shock. When my son went on his first date, the girl was almost an hour late. "It feels like I'm going to have a heart attack," he said as he waited.

When shock is activated, you'll go into sympathetic stimulation. You may feel wired or have difficulty sleeping soundly, which is normal when you enter the tunnel of the passage. The sleepless nights and the discomfort of sympathetic nervous system arousal are actually beneficial. They give you more time to go inside and find a resolution to your inner conflict.

The resolution to any conflict is passing through fear and choosing life. The attitude I take is a determined surrender. Once I know it's something I must do, I make the determination to show up and jump into it whatever may happen. A rite of passage can be like going through a high fever. It's uncomfortable but necessary to removing impurities from the body. Passing through fear and shock are inner initiations, rings of fire that leave you more alive.

How Does Facing Fear and Shock Help Growth?

Facing fear and shock shatters hypnosis.

John Upledger, a DO in Somato Emotional Release, relates treating a patient with seemingly incurable pelvic pain. Under therapy, she relived a past surgery. Apparently, the lead surgeon had finished the operation and asked his intern to stitch up the incision. When the intern finished, the surgeon said that the intern had done a sloppy job and that, if he had time, he'd do it over again. After the surgery, the woman developed an infection and healed poorly. During the operation, she was under anesthesia and completely unconscious, but remarkably, the subconscious suggestion that the intern's work was substandard must have depressed the immune system or somehow sabotaged her healing.

Bernie Siegel, MD, has been passionately teaching physicians about doctor hypnosis for decades. Siegel cautions physicians to watch every word, whether the patient is conscious or not. He observed that if a doctor had had a cancer patient opened up in surgery and commented that something didn't look good, the patient was slower to heal—if he healed at all.

An oncologist gave a woman nine months to live. She died nine months later on the prescribed day. Her daughter went back to the oncologist and asked him how he was able to predict the time of death so precisely. "It's my job to know," he said. "The years have made me an expert diagnostician." Even he didn't realize what was really happening. He'd hypnotized the woman.

When very sick patients go to a doctor, they are off-balance, out of the body, and in a compromised state of consciousness. The doctor, an authority figure, makes a pronouncement, which enters directly into the subconscious mind, and as a result, patients sometimes die just as the doctor said, and frequently on the exact day.

Don't let people hypnotize you unless you want to be hypnotized.

That's why I don't go to palm readers, psychics, or astrologists. I don't want anyone planting suggestions in my subconscious mind. I saw a psychic tell a woman her husband was cheating, so she divorced him. She had no proof, only the seed planted in her mind. I've seen astrologers tell clients that the next few months would be a dangerous or difficult time and that care needed to be employed. So the clients canceled planned trips and events. Some barely left the house during the "danger" period. This type of hypnosis is exactly what we do to ourselves.

We may not be aware of it, but our particular fear and shock patterns have us trained into a state of self-hypnosis that holds us back from living fully. I knew a Bolivian man who lived in America for his whole life and wanted to see his ancestors' home, but he was afraid of planes and rather stuck in his ways. He had a hard time getting out of his comfort zone, so there were many reasons he could never make the trip. I tried to convince him that the trip would serve as a rite of passage; it would have been the ticket out of prison. He would have returned triumphant, his self-imposed hypnotism shattered. That's why it's always such an alive thing to travel. You're set free from routine, cast into the stream of life with even something so simple as eating a meal: you don't know what you're going to eat or where. Everything has to be off the cuff.

We all subtly fall into habits around our fears. I like to call it "making a box." The box is the same as the ego egg, described earlier. The older we get, the more we live in the ruts of our minds. We develop routines: we must have our favorite pillow, schedules, medications, and accouterments to feel comfortable.

Routines and Habits

Routines seem good on paper. The body thrives on eating or exercising at regular times, and the mind adores a predictable routine. Aren't our routines what we've created as the best way to express our individuality? Yes and no. The trouble with routines is that the mind attaches and clings to them. Our routines and habits become our box. If you want to train a dog, you practice the same thing every day until it makes an impression on its mind. Once you have created the wrinkle in the dog's mind, it never forgets the trick. Habits create a wrinkle in the mind and become automatic.

Have you noticed that sometimes you drive your car without thinking where you're going? You arrive home mindlessly, the entire trip on automatic pilot. We often live our lives that way. We use routines as a crutch, a way to glide by without the effort of focusing conscious awareness. When receptivity is replaced by robotic automaticity, you lose spontaneity and aliveness. When people get old, their skin becomes wrinkly, but we might look to the relationship between age and how many wrinkles we have in the mind. The more routines and habits one has, the stronger the box and the less childlike wonder one has. But the box can be dismantled at any time.

The first time I went to Asia, my then-wife and I were having serious problems. I left anyway and arrived in Nepal for a six-week trip. Within two days, I became terribly sick with amoebic dysentery. While in the hallucination-like state of high fever, I thought about walking into my house and driving my car, but those thoughts seemed hazy and indistinct. My life back in the United States, even the problems, seemed very far away, almost as if they didn't exist. The old parable came to mind: If a tree falls in the forest and no one is there to hear it, does it make a sound? My life in America had been constructed with the mental energy I put into it, but since I'd been in Nepal, I'd put very little energy toward it. It was getting weaker and weaker. It struck me that if I stayed in Nepal, never to return, perhaps my life in America would fall down like an empty box. There would be nothing to hold it up. It would cease to exist.

Suggestions for Practice

Even if you have to do the same thing each day, approach it freshly. I love to do tai chi and yoga every morning, but there are always ways to approach them freshly and spontaneously.

In my little garden, nature is ever-changing, and I can experiment with moving my body slightly differently. Instead of performing robotically, I feel with the senses. Every time is different, almost as if it were the first time. Life lived from the receptivity of the true being is always fresh. Life lived from the wrinkles of the mind can be comforting, but it is far less alive.

I spent a summer in a Buddhist monastery. Everyone had daily work duty, and sometimes it was in the kitchen. We never knew what was going to be asked of us. We might have to cook for twenty people or one hundred and twenty. Often we were given a recipe, say for hummus, and told to make enough for forty people. The recipe, however, was for eight people, so we had to improvise. We made many mistakes and had to doctor dishes to make them palatable or else they ended up in the garbage. On top of that, no one told us where anything was. We had to find all the ingredients, pots, pans, dishes, and equipment. At first I thought the whole setup ridiculous and inefficient, but then I realized the entire thing was a calculated device, a method to break us out of our mental comfort zones. It was the most alive cooking I've ever experienced, and since that time I rarely follow a recipe or meticulously measure ingredients. Improvisation is less perfect but a lot more fun.

The To-do List

"It's my birthday today—I'm sixty," one of my patients said as he came into my office.

"How are you doing on your sixtieth birthday?" I asked him.

"You know, I'm doing fine, but I'll tell you one thing for sure."

"What's that?"

"I'm going to take a look at my to-do list and make sure everything I want to do gets done."

Good advice for anyone, at any age.

In the chapter on shock, I suggested looking over your life with an eye to the places where fear and shock hold you back. These are the dead places where the light doesn't circulate. These dead areas are precisely what must be passed through to accomplish your to-do list, your dreams in life. Remember, when you're on your deathbed, the only thing you will regret is not living—the things you were too afraid to do. Passing through them is a portal to aliveness. If you had to die right now, what would you wish you had done?

When You Know Your Heart—Take Action

When the voice of your heart is clear, follow it—physically. Doing is the physical rite of passage. If your heart wants love, go for it, risking even a thousand rejections. If you know your path and your goals, do it and let nothing deter you.

Pass Through

If you want to grow, life will always give you the opportunity to test your boundaries. When you have a chance to get out of your comfort zone, do so. Live on the edge. Every single time you pass through your self-imposed hypnosis, you become more alive. This does not mean to be a macho daredevil. Macho daredevils are frequently not centered in their bodies. They push blindly out of fear and may even have a subconscious death wish. Only through awareness will you see your own resistance and consciously choose life. Jump into life at every chance that's presented. I guarantee that every time you pass through your boundaries, you will be more alive.

The Part That Doesn't Change

As you pass through your personal rings of fire, remember to center yourself in your true being, the part that doesn't change.

The first time people go into a boxing or mixed-martial-arts gym, their palms are almost always sweaty. They see the ring and a couple of skilled guys sparring hard, and that makes them even more nervous. They might think something like, "People get hurt in there—I sure don't want to get my head taken off."

Many people have phobias about airplanes. When you're a passenger in a plane, you're cooped up and stuck in a tight place. If you're claustrophobic, it can easily activate shock. When the cabin door is locked, there's no turning back—especially because you aren't in control at all.

But the ultimate reality is that a boxing ring and the space inside an airplane are just space. Your inner self is the same in the ring, an airplane, or anyplace you go. You could be in the airplane and feeling claustrophobic and nervous, but the instant you shift from the mind to the part that doesn't change, you find peace and bliss. Even during the worst situations, try to find the place that doesn't change. It's always the same! Nothing can touch it. Gently watch as the mind becomes activated into fear and makes a mere space something larger than life.

It's Only a Thought

Another way to approach fear is to observe how it arises from the mind.

A friend of mine who's an emergency room physician described a woman who came in with pain and pressure in her chest and uncomfortable sensations running down her arms. The physician ran a bunch of tests, but the woman didn't have any discernible heart problems. The next evening she was back in the emergency room experiencing the same problem. Again he tested her, and again her heart was fine. Several days later she showed up with the same symptoms. After the tests came back negative for the third time, he told her that her symptoms were probably being caused by anxiety. In other words, they were in her head. Thoughts can be extremely powerful, such as the thought that triggers a panic attack, but they remain just thoughts, and a time comes when the entire process can be cut at the roots.

If you can get deeply into the observation process, pay attention to the thought that triggers fear or anxiety. It starts as an unconscious process. When someone is triggered on an airplane, it's not the close quarters in the airplane. The same person can sit in his car without panic. It's being out of control that touches the unconscious web of his shock. When the shock is activated, there will quickly be a thought, and from the thought the overwhelming feeling of panic ensues.

If we revisit the woman who thought she had heart trouble and kept going to the emergency room, we don't know how she was being unconsciously triggered into shock, but at some point the thought came that there was something wrong with her heart. And quick as a flash, her mind created pain and pressure in her chest, which only intensified her concerns.

The mind is capable of unlimited "what ifs," and it has tremendous power to activate fear. What if I get cancer, what if I lose all my money, what if I'm in pain, what if my wife leaves me, what if he doesn't find me attractive? If you as the witness can watch carefully when you find yourself triggered, look for the "what if" thought. When people come to me with a chronic worry, especially those who have explored their minds, I like to give them this practice. Remember: it's only a thought. The problem comes when we identify them. And, by now, you should know that chronic fear is not real. It's just an old, deeply ingrained psycho/emotional response that's affecting the nervous system. Just cut the thought process at the root and refuse to go there. All it takes is to switch awareness into the timeless part that doesn't change.

Another twist on this is what I call flushing the toilet. If, after you've explored your mind, you find yourself in the midst of a charged "what if" story, just abort it completely. Most people take the crap in their heads too seriously. They ruminate on it for hours and, in the process, tie their nerves into knots. Stop worshiping the crap in your mind. If you had a toilet bowl filled with feces, you wouldn't take out each piece and analyze it. You wouldn't let it sit there and smell up the house. Recognize that your thoughts are not serving you, not even the slightest bit. In fact they stink. Simply flush the toilet.

The ultimate benefit of a rite of passage is freedom from the boundaries of your mind. When you pass through a rite of passage, you come out the other side more relaxed and alive. You have broken through the egg and see yourself as a child of life. You're able to let go and trust life to take you under its wing, any time, anywhere. You stop trying to swim upstream and let the river of life take you where you need to go. When you are free from your mind, you are free.

PART 8

Surrender and Awakening

Chapter 17

Surrender

IN THE EXTERNAL WORLD, SURRENDER IS LOOKED ON AS weakness. We admire the warrior, in any walk of life, who never gives up. However, in the inner world, surrender is the real act of courage and the passage to oneness with life.

How to prepare for surrender? You don't need to. Life prepares you on the inside, until the inner flame grows so powerful that it burns off what you no longer need. It's not that the real self gets stronger—your real self is already perfect and does not need to be added to or subtracted from. The inner flame is an ever-increasing awareness and presence of itself. The more awareness you have of your real self, the more powerfully your heart beats in love and sincerity and the more you can see the chaos that the ego causes. You come to the understanding that you, the person, the ego mind, are the only obstacle to liberation.

Surrender and the Role of a Master

Traditionally, one learned the art of surrender under a master. Today the very word *master* raises suspicious eyebrows. Why allow a master to tell you what to do? Isn't it better to make your own decisions about your life? Having a master doesn't sound healthy and may even be dangerous. The potentially horrific results of surrendering to modern leaders have been noted with the cases of Charles Manson and Jim Jones.

There's a saying: when the student is ready, the teacher appears. But you never know what form the teacher will take. In some cases, life prepares us for surrender through a human teacher. Learning surrender with a master is natural because of the element of human love. If she is the right master for you, you will fall in love. Not romantically, of course, but you will love her deeply. When you love, your heart shows you the way to overcome fear and let go to trust. Trust leads to surrender.

Love makes you sensitive to the master. Your inner being perks up and takes notice of her inner being. You go deep inside her. Your hearts beat in the same rhythm like two tuning forks vibrating together. You become so attuned to her being that you go beyond words.

This happened to me with my kung fu master. For years I assisted him in teaching. I was so focused on him I could feel his vibration. I knew exactly what he wanted and when. There was no need for him to speak.

There's an old saying: Awakening can't be taught (truth isn't intellectual); it can't be bought (truth isn't for sale); it can only be caught. If you have bridged into your master through love and trust, you surrender to her guidance. Your inner being recognizes what she has attained. You are so focused on her that you perceive her state of consciousness. That's why awakening is called enlightenment. Your lamp is lighted from the inside. The being of the awakened master is the spark that ignites the consciousness of the student.

Even a poor master can yield results. And it doesn't matter what spiritual path you're on. It's the love and sincerity, the willingness to give up personal control, that make an impression on the soul of the universe.

Surrender Without a Master

It's not a problem if you don't have a master. Ultimately, surrender is the secret key. If you surrender to life, life will direct you. If you surrender to your inner guru (your own true self), your heart will speak and you'll be given all the direction you need. If you completely surrender to a rosebush, you will be surprised. The rosebush will start talking to you. People think the story of Moses and the burning bush is just some fairy tale, but I'm pretty certain it's based on fact and was probably part of Moses's awakening. Moses walked up the mountain in a state of complete trust and surrender, and life spoke to him. The fire around the bush was probably Moses's witnessing of the unified energy of life (love).

All of life is ready to teach those whose ears, eyes, and hearts are open. I used to run every day in the forest and liked to make a slight detour to visit an ancient fir tree. I'd put my arms around the massive trunk and just listen. The most profound words of wisdom poured into my heart. Over a lifetime, I've had many allies in nature that have proffered sublime teachings.

Surrender Is of the Ego

The final act of surrender entails not the surrender of the real self but the giving up of the false self. When you let go of all control, the real self merges effortlessly; the true self returns to its natural state of oneness with life. The illusion of separateness is over. You know what you are.

On the road to surrender, especially when you're getting close, there appears to be an interface, a fight between your ego and real self. But this is just the mind's desperate attempt to keep itself in the driver's seat, and it's certainly part of the process. I call this stage the mind's last stand.

The Mind's Last Stand

Finding the core and passing through rites of passage are deeply profound and life-changing experiences, but the mind has been in control for a long time, and it will use all its power to stay there. This stage, the metaphorical cliff of surrender, could be called the last hurrah of the mind. The ego hangs on like a pit bull. Serious meditators frequently come to this point. They're sitting in peace and touch upon the void, a deep nothingness. All of a sudden, fear arises. They feel as if they'll cease to exist. As soon as fear comes, they go right back into the mind again. It's ironic: they've arrived at the door of no mind, the very state they've been reaching toward from the beginning, but now that they've arrived they turn back.

Strange how, in this stage, the mind seems to be acting up again, reasserting itself even more intensely. You might think you've passed through everything already, but in the mind's last stand, you seem to have regressed. You may experience the mind as a drill sergeant. You'll see how you've jumped to the mind's voice your entire life. You long for peace and stillness, but every thought causes tension—even the good ones—because every thought is an effort, a disturbance of stillness, a whipping up of brain waves, an irritation of nerves. You come to the startling realization that every time you pass judgment, you're out of the body. Every time you enter into any thought at all, the gem of pure consciousness diminishes.

You see that thought truly is a movement to a different world—the mind world—and these worlds are limitless. You understand why shamans call it going to a different dimension. The more shock and trauma one has, the deeper the grooves of the mental knot that's been formed and the stronger the pull into the well-worn rut of old emotions.

If you stay with the process, it's more and more difficult to shunt. There's no place to go. You may dance or exercise to attempt to hold your mind together; engage the mind by thinking of songs, fantasies, or long-forgotten memories; or even try to meditate and stop the thoughts, but now the very effort of trying causes a marked uneasiness. You want to run, but at the same time you are infinitely weary. The cliff is beckoning closer.

Waves of fear may flit in and out. If your mind—what you've always believed is you—is so crazy, what do you have to count on? How will you live in the world? What will happen if you go insane? (Fear of losing the mind has always been closely associated with this stage.) But here you can't forget that the ego is on the run and feeling very threatened. The ego has its own survival consciousness. Like a drowning man will fight to get to the surface to save his life, the ego desperately clings to dear life. It must create chaos; it must constantly move and spin like a top; it must try to divide everything. It must fight to control or let go, and if it lets go, that's exactly like death to the ego, and it's terrifying.

If you stay with it, allow it to happen, you may experience a moment of fear. You may feel helpless, as if you're falling apart and moving into the void where no one can help you. In this place, one may desperately pray for help—even an atheist. But no one will answer except your own being; this step must be taken solo. There is a sense of urgency. In a last-ditch effort to escape, consciousness may attempt to flee the body as fast as it can, as it has always done in the past. And the faster you try to get away, the more panic there is because you get farther away from your center. Being away from home has always been the root cause of uneasiness.

You may try everything you've practiced up to this point, focusing on the feeling and attempting to bring yourself deep inside the shock, you may strain to hold yourself in the body, but this time nothing works. Even bringing yourself to the core isn't enough to bring peace. It's all effort, and every effort is now disturbing. This is the moment of truth. If you're not ready to surrender, you will find a way to shunt. That's why preparation is ultimately the same in all paths. If you haven't untied the inner knots and penetrated your shock, you probably won't surrender.

If you are prepared, it dawns on you what's happening and why. This is what all the training has been about. Immediately, your inner awareness comes back and settles in the body. Now you are standing on the very edge of the cliff. You let go of all effort and surrender into the unknown. Instantly, all tension vanishes and is replaced with absolute bliss and peace. You have jumped into the stream of life and are part of it. Only your true self remains as awareness.

Part of the Whole

When you see and feel that the life force within you—the real you—is the same as is in a dog, a plant, a rock, a tree, the air, or another person, when you see and feel that life, *prana*, *yuan qi*, God, the unified field, or whatever you wish to call it, is literally a soup of shimmering, pulsating energy, you'll never be the same. Its substance is love, and that's what you are. Your heart opens in earnest, and peace and ecstasy floods your being. The only word that comes close is *thanks*.

When you know that everything isn't merely connected but one, it changes your entire outlook. You know for certain—it's not an abstract philosophy—that whatever you do to help or hurt any part of life affects the whole.

In a marriage, there can't be a winner and a loser. The notion is ridiculous. When a couple are together, there's an energetic joining; they literally become one. The husband can't win if the wife loses. It's just not possible. If she loses, at some point he—they—will also lose. Only win-win solutions work in a marriage. What enhances well-being for one will enhance it for the entire family system. It's the same with life. An individual can't gain against the whole. Every being is like a teabag in the soup of life. It leaves its essence. Whatever you do leaves its mark. The old yoga credo "May all be happy, may all be healthy, may all know kindness" is burned deeply into your heart and is even extended to yourself.

Your vision shifts away from the personal and toward the good of the whole. You can't help but be brimming with compassion for all of life. You think about how you can make the world a better place, and the shift changes the power of your vision. It's a strange phenomenon: when the individual tries to satisfy his own desires, the result is limited precisely because of the ego's separateness. However, when one attempts to satisfy the desires of the whole, the entire universe conspires to fulfill it.

After surrender into oneness, people often report being in their bodies for what feels like the first time in their lives. Thought waves are naturally attenuated—their amplitude and frequency decrease. The physical body becomes a more comfortable home. Clear consciousness settles and takes root. This is the true union of the inner and outer selves. Not figuratively or intellectually but in a literal, energetic sense. When the inner and physical selves are integrated, one in harmonious relationship with the other, you can enjoy all the gifts life has to offer. This is spirit made flesh and the true power of now.

The Paradox of Surrender

It's either jump or not. And yet the jump usually comes when mental control and manipulation of life are exhausted. When we have reached the endpoint of effort, surrender happens, much like the technique of tensing the muscles before they let go. But in truth, surrender is so simple and natural that we do it all the time. Being part of the whole is ridiculously natural. All you have to do is be aware. After my own experience, I remembered the many times I'd disappeared without even knowing it. And that's the problem: we just aren't aware of what's happened.

When I was a little kid, probably about two years old, I went outside with my pail and shovel on a bright spring day. I sat on the grass and looked around, not thinking about anything. I felt the energy of the sun, the earth, the sky, the trees, and each blade of grass. Deep in my being, I knew that I, the alive part inside me, was of the same substance as nature. I just sat for a few minutes spreading out, the boundaries between me and life eroding. I felt total bliss. At the time, I had no words or reference point for the experience.

At six or seven years old, I'd hang out with the family cat under a bush and watch the bugs on the backs of the leaves. I'd just zone out into nothingness and experience union with nature and all life. At ten or twelve, I would sometimes just let myself go, even around others. One time at summer camp, as I ate dinner in an open-air dining room, I stared into space and zoned out. It felt as if my body melted away, and I was in pure bliss. People thought there was something wrong with me; they called my name and shook me to make sure I was okay. I was simply dropping the mind and experiencing the unified love of life. It was so natural it didn't seem special at all. When my mind clicked in, I forgot about all about it.

We all do this many times a day: slip into no mind and begin to blend with the whole. Those are some of the most pleasurable moments of living—if you let it happen with a lover, it's insanely profound. Two individuals are no longer making love; you and the other are gone. All that remains is the love. But when the mind starts moving again, we snap back into our separate selves, which brings us instantly back to the mental world of division and judgment, our own personal prison. The trick is to see the difference deeply, to make both states conscious. When the eyes of your true self see clearly, surrender and awakening become a way of life. The true self has taken the driver's seat.

You can disappear into the sea of life any time, anywhere, and without fear. The instant you enter into no mind, the boundaries between you and life disappear. You become nothing and everything. You gain energy because your nervous system relaxes and lets in the energy of life. You are literally fed by life, which is why some yogis and meditators eat very little. They've learned the trick of absorbing cosmic energy.

In a documentary on the Kumbha Mela, a spiritual festival held every twelve years in India, the Dalai Lama gave a talk to a mostly Hindu audience and said something like: "You

Hindus believe in atman (soul), but we Tibetan Buddhists believe in non-atman ... but who cares (with a laugh)."

After we've experienced surrender, the non-atman seems closer to truth. We really are nothing, but at the same time we are a part of everything—which is also nothing, but a nothing so full of life it is indescribable. If you experience surrender, you'll know what separateness and oneness are, why consciousness leaves the body every time the mind moves, and where it goes. See for yourself what happens to clear consciousness when the mind moves even slightly. You'll know why heaven and hell exist within you, right here and now.

With Surrender Comes Spontaneity

A free woman is naturally spontaneous. She's unfettered by entanglements that steal awareness. Entangled in the mind, we are cloudy and unsure of ourselves. Hence the need to adopt rules and value systems. If a religion or scripture gives us the correct formula to live by, we can memorize it and know the "right" thing to do in any situation. But as said in Chapter 7, having a recipe book on how to live life properly is a poor substitute for being aware.

Trungpa Rinpoche shocked the Buddhist world when he said that one needs to be careful sneaking up behind and messing around with a bodhisattva (an enlightened one). Trungpa warned that the bodhisattva might turn around and punch you in the face. He might break your bones and even kill you. Many in the Buddhist world freaked out because they had been taught that nonviolence was the proper way. A good Buddhist shouldn't hurt any living creature, much less violently destroy another human being. Trungpa liked to shock people into awareness. He was trying to say that an awakened person is unpredictable; you never know what she will do. One who is free flows along with life, in a state of awareness. She trusts herself to spontaneously do what is necessary in any given moment.

If something needs effort, you put forth effort. If someone needs help, you give it, or perhaps not, depending on the circumstances life presents. Even the words you use are not rehearsed or planned. When I'm called to give a speech or a talk in public, I never rehearse or read from a script. The talk may not be polished, but at least it's real, and that carries power. Words seem to come out by themselves, and you can trust that they are right. Even when they seem to go wrong, the whole ultimately turns out right.

The Echo from the Heart

There's a way to double-check this heart-centered spontaneity. The heart receives perceptions directly from life. From the heart the vision goes to the mind. If, instead of analyzing the energy after it enters into thought, you send whatever your inner heart told you back to the heart, the heart will immediately echo back a confirmation. You will know if it's right by the distinct feeling that the return echo brings.

Suggestions for Practice

Surrender into Sleep

Sleep has been called a little death, and it is. Every time you go to sleep, there comes a time when you actually do let go. If you continue to think, it will be difficult to fall asleep. When you're lying in bed, consciously let go completely as if it's really time to die.

Surrender into Every Moment

The mind resists life, like trying to drive a car with a foot on the gas pedal and the other foot on the brake. That's what we do when the ego mind worries and ruminates about what's going to happen next. The ego worries how good it will look, what others will think, and all manner of "what ifs." The ego can't really help itself, because it's desperately trying to control the uncontrollable. Every time the mind stresses, however, your nervous system jumps, and stress chemicals are produced that act as an irritant to the health of your body. What if you could just let go into life, trust and flow with it? If one could surrender to every moment, the brakes and resistance to life would dissolve.

Surrender into the Now

Much of life is a desperate journey to reach a goal. Joy and satisfaction have prerequisites. We must have the right relationship, job, education, and bank account. Because we spend so much time chasing future phantoms, life becomes stressful. It's easy to project to a more pleasant time or place, as when you fantasize about when work will be over and you can do what you want, but then you miss what's happening in the now.

The ultimate avoidance is to put off living fully in the here and now in hopes of everlasting paradise in heaven. Projecting hope for a better future, especially one after you're dead, is a delusion. If you look carefully, consciousness perpetuates itself, even into death. If you can't live now, don't fool yourself that things will radically change in the afterlife.

Sometimes older people give up on projections and come to a place of acceptance. When young, maybe they burned to change the world and make themselves special. They had aspirations: to be rich, find love, achieve enlightenment, or whatever. Maybe they achieved them or maybe not, but now—fifty or sixty years later—they realize they aren't going to change much. They are what they are. And the world hasn't become all that different. It goes on. Finally they can accept themselves and life as it is, without prerequisites, hopes, or goals.

Don't wait. Find peace, love, and joy in the present. Dance, celebrate, and live now! Waiting for a vacation or the weekend when you get off work isn't going to help in the deeper sense. If you're stressed and miserable now, that imprints your nervous system and will be perpetuated in the future. Even if retired and sitting on the beach, you may still be stressed and miserable.

Cardiologist Stephen Sinatra, MD, cites research suggesting that the most common time to have a heart attack is Monday morning. Arrhythmias peaked on Monday mornings and, not surprisingly, decreased on Saturdays and Sundays. The outpouring of stress hormones, such as cortisol and adrenaline, may trigger the attack. Some researchers believe this pattern may continue even after retirement. It seems that the habitual stress and dread of going to work may permanently imprint the nervous system and wreak havoc in the body.

What's happening right now is the only reality. If you're bone-tired, bored, or struggling through stressful times, don't fantasize into the future; sink deeply into whatever's happening and see what is here for you right now in the present. Whatever you're doing, find the inner part of you that's always in bliss. Even the worst moments can be appreciated by seeing from the part of you that doesn't change. Find bliss, light, and love—your center—now.

Chapter 18

Seeing with Different Eyes

THE TRUE SELF SEES WITH DIFFERENT EYES FROM THE mind, and seeing with these inner eyes has tremendous ramifications for every aspect of your life.

Stop Fighting

With surrender and awakening, the urge to fight and create conflict vanishes. You stop fighting with others. You don't have to be right anymore.

Cleaning Up Bad Blood Is Another Form of Freedom

You'll naturally want to clean up any tangles that may exist between you and anyone else. Grudges, bad blood, and misunderstandings keep you energetically entangled. Apologize when necessary, and let others vent their anger to move their feelings. When I apologized to my first wife, I simply took responsibility for what I'd done in our relationship. I wasn't interested in her owning up to her part—and she didn't. She got angry and asked me why I'd acted the way I did. I replied that I'd been immature. Really, I'd been unconscious.

In my case, my ex felt better and accepted my apology. But even if the other person isn't clear (free from grudges, resentment, or bad blood), at least you'll have done what you can.

In the process of walking through the valley of death, you've painstakingly observed the ego's tendency to create conflict. Conflict is food for the ego, and the ego literally gets fat on it. With surrender, you no longer engage with another's ego. With your true self in charge, you have no inclination to enter into skirmishes with others' egos. Only an idiot would purposely crash his car into another vehicle—both vehicles will be damaged. And that's why a mature martial artist avoids fighting at all costs. Yet most people will butt their ego heads against each other at the drop of a hat. When you've surrendered, ego is a mere shadow. Even if someone tries to engage you, you remain nonreactive. You can't have a tug of war unless both parties hold the rope; now you simply avoid picking it up.

Stop Fighting with Yourself

Even more common than fighting with others is engaging in an inner struggle with ourselves. By now you've seen the no-saying voice, the small voice, the insecure, unlovable, not-good-enough voice, and other voices of the ego so many times that you don't take them seriously. You can laugh at yourself. You know that you—your ego identity—is messed up, but it no longer bothers you in the slightest. Now you can even become friends with the ego. After all, it has been meticulously formed by destiny and has been the perfect vehicle for you. The ego has been the cocoon, and surrender leads to metamorphosis.

Stop Fighting with Life

You've seen how the mind is like a claw, grasping and hanging madly on, desperately trying to control the circumstances of its separateness. But with surrender comes the knowing that life always has you under its wing and takes you where you need to go. Like a vast river whose current can't be navigated, you see the utter futility of trying to control and manipulate the wild current of life. Life is perfect in that it provides the circumstances for growth in every way, and you learn to let go and trust it. You let life take you where it may.

I recently read an article written by a psychologist who questioned the philosophy—the one obviously put forth in this book—that says one must take responsibility for everything that happens, as if on some level we choose and create what happens to us. Some calamity had occurred in her life and had left her thinking: *I didn't choose this. No part of me wanted this to happen, nor did I create it.* She was a good person. She'd done nothing to deserve the amount of pain that life dished out. I agree we may not choose something on a conscious level—certainly, our ego didn't choose pain—but on the deepest level, maybe we did choose to grow. Life is too profound to understand fully.

I have a pet theory: truth may be far from what it appears to be. For example, take two men—one a drug addict on skid row and the other a well-to-do leader who seemingly has everything going for him. He's healthy and prosperous, and he has a great relationship. The status quo would judge the leader to be good and the addict bad. However, what if before the two men were born, the leader had decided he was too weary to keep pressing on and made the decision that he needed to rest for a few lifetimes. So then he finds himself in an easy life he can coast through. But because he's doing so well, he's forgotten that he'd just wanted to take it easy. He's teaching others, thinking he's found the secret to a good life. Meanwhile, the drug addict may have said, "Just bring it on. I'll face anything I need to." On the outside, it looks like the leader is more advanced than the addict, but who really knows?

The point is that ultimately our lives are not mistakes or accidents. Your inner wounds and circumstances are not problems but rather necessary vehicles that brought you to the place where you are. Everything, even the bad stuff, helped to make you who you had to be and may very well turn into blessings.

Having children matures one quickly. Single people of all ages are often rather self-centered. It's natural. All they have to worry about is their own interests. Nothing is as important as their own lives. But to have a child, a woman holds life in her body. She builds the child's body from the very marrow of her blood and bones. Every single time a woman gets pregnant, it's a matter of life and death. There's no guarantee the baby or the mother will survive, but she surrenders to it. It's no mistake that women birth babies—women are ultimately far braver than men. A man thinks he's hot stuff to fight or go to war, but women are the true warriors. A woman looks death in the eye every time she gets pregnant.

Both men and women grow more quickly if they are loving parents. The heart opens to learn sacrifice. Their love for the child transforms self-centeredness into something bigger. It is always love that transforms, and love for life is often born through pain.

After working with thousands of people, I've noticed that those who've gone through the most suffering are some of the most beautiful people. Life may dish out tremendous pain, leaving grievous wounds and deep scars on the heart. Some people protect those scars as they retreat further into the safety of the egg. Others endure the same pain and suffering—even horrific experiences—and somehow open the heart and burst into freedom. Some of the greatest humanitarians have been seasoned through pain. Pain pulls a switch, making people parents to life, parents who devote themselves to alleviating human suffering wherever they can. It can be tempting to envy those who seem comfortable—almost callous or insensitive—but with consciousness and passing through to the other side, all our sensitivities turn to advantages. The obstacles you overcame on your road to awakening will provide the insights needed to help others in their transformation.

It's not only our light that attracts us to others but also our darkness. Our wounds have a resonance with others who possess the same wounds. We attract, ultimately, to heal each other. Every person who crosses your path has some of the same wounds you do, but because you are still embroiled in your ego, you fail to see that you're naturally attracting others in the same boat—and because you are unconscious, you can't help them. When you've passed through your own valley of death, you'll know what medicine you used to heal your own illness, and you'll be aware of the phenomenon of attraction. All those who cross your path have a certain resonance with you. They possess a similar piece of your wounding. When you can feel that, you'll naturally be able to help them to navigate to a clearer place.

Seeing What You Want

In the very first chapter, I asked the question "What do you want?" Most people will answer from the ego, but until you get to the core, you may not really know the answer.

If you want to drive somewhere but don't know how to get there, you can still get in your car and take a ride. Maybe you have a grand adventure, get lost, break down, get mugged, or discover some interesting sights. Many people go through life without an inner map. If they do have one, it's someone else's, or a version of society's ideal. People comment that I must be proud to have made it through so many years of school. I tell them that doing is easy. Once I knew what I wanted, I just put one foot in front of the other and kept walking. Knowing what you truly want is often the hard part. That's why receiving a vision is crucial.

I use the word *vision* only because there's no better way to describe the phenomenon of inner knowing. It may appear that we, as individuals, decide what we want to accomplish. However, in the deepest sense, we don't do or create anything. Life decides what will be manifested through whom. Gandhi, Mozart, and Michael Jordan were not accidents. Life chooses the vehicle that will most efficiently bring a particular gift or message to the whole.

Once I asked a famous musician how he could possibly compose such fine works of art. How did he create them? He was very humble. "I can't take one bit of credit for it," he said. "I heard the music in my head and simply wrote it down."

Inner knowing doesn't come from the mind; it's born from no mind. When free from the mind, visions seem to download directly to the heart. They're a gift from life itself, from the whole to its molecules. Unlike the mind, which has conflicting voices, the heart has only one. The heart just knows. It doesn't matter if your vision is large or small. Some visions might take many years to harvest, such as being a doctor or an engineer. Others are simply flashlights on the path so you can see the next step. Either way, the clear knowing in your heart should never be turned away from. Indigenous peoples always sought a vision. Once they received one, they spent the rest of their lives walking that vision or until they received another.

When I came near death, I identified three things that were important to me: giving and receiving love, doing what I came here to do, and leaving the world a better place in some way. Actually, the second two are extensions of the first. Doing what you came here to do is to find the place where you can give and receive the most love, and how else will we leave the world better? To grow, one continually seeks to refine one's personal platform, your place in the world through which you come into contact with others. Refining your platform might mean changing your job to one you enjoy more, writing a book, or doing volunteer work—anything that allows you to give and receive love more efficiently and share yourself at the deepest level. You might say knowing how to refine the platform of giving and receiving love is the vision. It aligns your heart and soul with what you do in life. But refining your platform is not doing—it's a following, a receptivity to life. It's being yourself and letting the current of life take you where it will. The urge in your own heart whispers there is another step to take in life. If you don't listen to the voice of your heart you crimp your own inner flow and become older in spirit.

Having a true vision takes much of the stress and tension away from the work of doing and is the basis of Lao Tzu's famous expression "to do without doing." When your vision burns like a flame in your heart, it takes little effort to bring about. Actualizing your vision is so natural and compelling that it seems you have no choice, and so it becomes effortless.

After you've surrendered your tormenting ego, simply trust life. It's not necessary to do more. You don't have to reprogram yourself to have correct thoughts, try to be a better person, or do anything at all. The emptier and quieter you are, the better. Your own heart knows exactly what needs to be done.

Seeing through Addiction

Some dark meditations, like some love affairs, have to be taken to the bitter end before we see that the relationship can never work. Only then can one let go. Awakening often brings you to that place. Only when perceiving life with the real self can we see the ramifications of our habits and addictions. It's a question of reality, a seeing with the eyes of death. The clear part that never dies knows this lifetime is finite; only this part can understand clearly enough to choose peace over chaos.

A healthy lifestyle comes not from morals, ethics, or standards of excellence but from deep awareness. When awake and conscious, you see the full chain of energetic events as they unfold like one domino striking against another. Though there may still be times when it's tempting to turn to your addiction, you see the entire cycle it will cause. You'll know each trigger—how and why you turn to a dark meditation when your mind is overwhelmed. It was once an unconscious protection, a survival mechanism, but now it throws you off balance. You'll see, in advance, the falling off the wagon, the zone-out, the feeling bad about it, and the promising never to do it again. Most of all, you'll see the wasted time and inner chaos it creates.

At eighteen I had a job parking cars at a restaurant. One night after work, a waiter named Benson, probably in his late thirties, and I got together for a few beers. It turned out he was gay and trying his best to seduce me. I nipped his advances in the bud by telling him I preferred women, and the conversation turned to my upcoming trip to California.

"California," he said. "I could hook you up with a friend of mine—her name's Ramona. She's a real wild lady who'll show you a good time." These were the seventies, and the days of easy sex and sixties partying were still in full swing. "Far out," I said and took her number. After settling in at my hotel, I called Ramona.

"Hi," I said. "Benson gave me your number and told me to look you up." "Benson, huh?" she said. After a little small talk, she asked, "How old are you, anyway?"

"Eighteen," I said.

Ramona sighed and was silent for a long moment. "Okay," she said, "I guess you'd better bring a toothbrush"—implying, of course, that I'd at least be staying the night.

"Fantastic," I said. "How do I get to your place?"

She gave me directions, I jumped in the shower, gathered a few things for the night, and put on a clean shirt. As I stood looking at myself in the mirror, the phone rang. It was Ramona.

"I'm sorry, I just can't do this anymore," she said and hung up.

She had said yes automatically, and in the past she would have simply gone through with it. But now she was probably a woman in her late thirties. She'd done this so many times and knew exactly what it would entail. I'm not judging myself or her or saying what we were considering was wrong. It's just that there comes a time when one finally wakes up and sees clearly. If something is causing chaos and sabotaging one's joy of being, one refuses to particulate any longer. Our inner eyes see the absolute ridiculousness of hurting ourselves.

When death is on your shoulder, you're aware that every instant is precious and that this particular life is finite and fleeting; you don't know how long you have. You'll clearly see how a particular habit is causing inertia: it's keeping you unconscious and out of your body. It's holding you in stasis, preventing you from doing what you want in life, whatever it may be. The ramifications of the dark meditation are clear, and the price may simply be too high. The bottom line is that you don't want to be asleep or separate anymore. You choose peace, which is true health, over chaos. You choose freedom over slavery. The instant the inner self sees clearly, it's an "aha" moment and addictions fall away.

Seeing with the Inner Senses

When the inner self takes root in the physical body, previously sleeping inner senses come to life. One may become clairvoyant, which is the opening of the inner sight. Perhaps one's inner ears, smell, touch, or direct knowing comes to life. However, these are not really powers at all but the normal gifts we all possess. They are your birthright. Not everyone develops each one of the inner senses, but everyone has them. It's up to the individual to discover and cultivate his or her own particular gifts.

If the sense of knowing is developed, people think someone is a mind reader. Buddha was sometimes called a crystal mirror because his mind was as silent as still water. No distortion colored his lenses, so whatever came within his vision was reflected clearly. If a man sat in front of him, Buddha saw to the depths of his soul. This clarity can be useful for helping others because one can see the truth of what people are doing energetically. They themselves may not know—they are approaching the problem with their egos—but someone with a silent mind can see to the depths.

Love

There are three colossal surrenders in life: real death, surrender of the ego, and surrender into love. Any surrender has the potential to be difficult, which is why we protect ourselves from it. Many people don't let themselves really love, because it's too dangerous to be so out of control. If you truly open your heart, it can be crushed. Out of fear, most people seek subtle or not-so-subtle manipulations and controls, which ultimately destroy relationships.

The surrendered know that life is eventually about saying good-bye to everything and everyone you love, but they are ready to take the risk to love fearlessly for love's sake. They have no choice; their hearts are open. When one stops fighting, one has no desire to control; one keeps his energy from assaulting another's, and so love blooms joyously.

After surrender, you know that you are a drop of pure love.

You don't have to be anything but who you are and share yourself freely.

Suggestions for Practice

Freedom, at least for me, remains a gift that has to be constantly won with awareness. My practice is to see life through the eyes of the real self the entire waking day. If my mind tries to reassert itself back into the old ruts of fear, desire, "what ifs," and fantasies—which immediately take me scrambling back to the false self—I watch with amusement.

Greeting the Small Self

When Paul Greenbaum (my ego identity) comes on the scene because someone stepped on his tail and he judges, worries, wants to be seen, gets his feelings hurt, or engages in some other typical ego activity, I observe it closely, shrug my shoulders, smile, and say to myself, "There's Paul Greenbaum again." It's just a simple good-natured acknowledgment. After surrender, I simply can't take my false self seriously anymore. I know Paul Greenbaum far too well for that.

Mind or No Mind

It's a mistake to think that one goes into permanent no mind. It's the nature of the mind to move. Diagnostic equipment has been hooked up to meditation masters to measure the degree of their brain activity, and even the most accomplished meditation expert still has thoughts every few seconds. The brain of a meditation master may have activity, but there's little charge or reaction to the thought.

When I need to use the mind for a specific purpose, I use it. But no matter how much my mind is engaged, clear consciousness is so close and familiar that it's never absent for long. Because my real self is captain of the ship, my days are spent in wonder and contentment, and although I am a citizen of the one, I delight in the magnificent, bittersweet play of duality.

Postscript
The Need for Unlearning

THERE'S AN OLD SAYING IN CHINA: TREAT A CHILD LIKE A god for the first five years and like a slave thereafter. The idea is to let the child knows she's loved, build a healthy self-image (ego), and bolster her self-esteem during her formative years. But then at the tender age of five, the youngster gets a dose of ego-squashing reality. You can see this type of training in the kung fu movies, where the disciple is always getting his ego crushed.

I think five is way too early to begin breaking down the ego. It may sound like a contradiction to the philosophy outlined in this book, but children and teens should be built up as much as possible. Still, wouldn't it be nice if children were taught about the inner self, no mind, and how to be more aware? Kids should be encouraged to be their own unique selves and not a clone of anyone else or society at large.

Programs for Children

I'm developing programs for children and teenagers. Please contact me for information on rite-of-passage vision quests, ecstasy yoga, and Brazilian jujitsu camps. During each of these programs, young people will go inside and face themselves in various ways. They will have group support and be able to process their inner conflicts if they so choose.

Vision Quests

Traditional vision quests are done without food and many times without water. After preparations, one sits on the land without electronics or any distractions. The lack of food quickly stirs one up and into a non-ordinary state of consciousness. Modified vision quests can also be performed with very light, simple food and water, but no distractions except a pad of paper for writing or drawing and/or a musical instrument. It's going inside and facing the fears of the mind that's the true rite of passage.

Ecstasy Yoga Camp

Ecstasy yoga develops the energetic body, bringing health, vitality, and joy and ultimately leading to surrender. It's a companion to the path outlined in this book. After many years practicing yoga, *qigong*, and meditation, I found that when you combine elements of all three, you can potentiate the results. Ecstasy yoga contains simple, practical tools that will help anyone. If children learn this practice when young, they will have practices to ground them throughout their lives.

Brazilian Jujitsu Camps

Martial arts in themselves can be a rite of passage. For some young people, it is the right thing at the right time, especially for kids with raging hormones and focus and disciplinary problems. The very same child who is rebellious to parental or any other authority respects the martial arts teacher because his or her skills are superior. Martial arts provide the perfect outlet for aggression and a positive way to develop the mind and body. They are especially beneficial when the teacher comes from the heart and looks to mentor. If one stays in the martial arts for any length of time, out of necessity one faces oneself deeply.

Brazilian jujitsu is unique in the martial arts world because it is a gentle art that requires an incredible degree of skill and finesse but is also a full-contact sport. It's by virtue of the tap (submission), a verbal or physical signal that one wants to stop, that we can use full contact safely, unlike in most other martial arts. The degree of combat experience one develops with such full-contact fighting brings genuine confidence in one's skills.

Brazilian jujitsu camps can be combined with a vision quest and or yoga/meditation intensives for an unforgettable experience that will nourish your child for his or her entire life.

Author's Note

Lao Tzu, the legendary founder of Taoism, supposedly said: "As soon as you speak of truth, you've already lost it."

Indeed, words are mental constructs that reach only to the mind. Words are inadequate, and yet I've written an entire book of words. My hope is that the words will create an echo, which will penetrate into the heart--were the journey begins.

About the Author

PAUL GREENBAUM began martial arts, yoga, and meditation at a young age. In his thirties he became a chiropractor, acupuncturist, and massage therapist. Although he had plenty of tools to help his patients, some didn't get well because inner conflicts were disturbing their mental and emotional peace. Trying to help those that didn't respond as well as he would've liked, led to many years of study with esoteric psychologists, clairvoyants, shamans in the Amazon, and doctors and healers from around the world.

The most important lesson he learned is that true health is freedom. When the body, mind, and emotions are free flowing and in harmony, the heart opens, and the spirit blossoms naturally, without effort. Dr. Paul Greenbaum truly committed to making this world a better place, one person at a time.

If you are interested in his programs or wish to speak to Paul Greenbaum, contact him at:

https://www.timetrade.com/book/KTNXS

www.ingramcontent.com/pod-product-compliance
Lightning Source LLC
Chambersburg PA
CBHW030437300426
44112CB00009B/1040